AF797838

The Connecticut DUI Guide

By

Attorney Jay Ruane

Attorney Teresa DiNardi

Edited by

Jennifer Sanfilippo

Printed in the United States of America

Different Middle Initial, LLC

ISBN 978-0-9965631-2-3

Chapters

Foreword

You are probably reading this book because you need help. If this is the case, you have come to the right place. We wrote this book for one purpose: to help our clients understand exactly what happens when they are charged with a DUI.

Our interest in writing this book was the experience of representing thousands of clients in Connecticut for DUI charges. Too often, clients are confused while dealing with their brush with the criminal justice system.

By investigating so many cases, and carefully questioning our clients, police officers, and witnesses, we learned that many people need more information about how the process works and how they can obtain a better result.

The criminal justice system is strongly favored towards the government, which has pressure from groups such as Mothers Against Drunk Driving (MADD) demanding that legislators, prosecutors, and judges deal harshly with people accused of driving under the influence. There is no doubt that alcohol has played a role in many motor vehicle accidents, injuries, and even deaths. However, the Constitution does provide rights to all persons charged with crimes. Despite the best efforts of some to remove these rights, they still exist albeit with the odds in favor of the government. Understand that the government has an easier time convicting a person accused of DUI today than at any other time in American history.

Please keep in mind that this book was written for non-lawyers. It represents a large amount of our knowledge regarding this area of Connecticut law and is adapted specifically for regular people like you who are caught in a confusing criminal justice system. A clearer understanding of the process is the aim of this book, and hopefully its serves you well.

Throughout the course of the book, we will guide you through the process facing you in the coming weeks and months ahead. Most importantly, it is necessary to state the obvious: this book is not a substitute for a trained, licensed, and experienced DUI lawyer like one at Ruane Attorneys. We may be biased, but we encourage you to retain an attorney who focuses his or her practice on defending people accused of DUI.

Most likely you are anxious or perhaps even scared about your arrest and the implications for your family, reputation, and your career. The allegation of driving under the influence of drugs or alcohol is not one that most people want to face alone. In this book, we will show you what we have learned during our careers practicing law, that hope is not a strategy.

Before we get any farther, let us introduce ourselves. We are attorneys Jay Ruane and Teresa DiNardi, partners at Ruane Attorneys. You can learn more about us and what we can do to help you here.

Attorney Jay Ruane

My name is attorney Jay Ruane, and I have been practicing DUI law in the state of Connecticut for nearly twenty years. While I was growing up in Connecticut, my father was a local criminal defense lawyer. I watched him go to work every day defending the rights of people just like you and me. He took enormous pride in his job, and he taught me the importance of protecting the rights of every man and woman. My father firmly believed that it is the job of the criminal defense lawyer to check the power of the court and make sure that the laws are followed during the prosecution process. This is a belief that I saw in action every day, and one that I came to adopt as my own. This way of viewing the world led me to my career as a lawyer.

In 1998, I graduated from law school and took a job as a public defender in the Bridgeport Courthouse. At this time in my career, I worked on hundreds of pending DUI cases at any given point. But instead of crumbling under the pressure, I came to thrive on it.

Due to the amount of time that I spent in court, I honed my skills as a public speaker and came to love being in the courtroom, unlike many attorneys who find that they are intimidated by it. I spent hours in the law libraries pouring over complex and obscure laws and scientific articles in order to find defenses for my clients. And I developed a highly organized system for handling cases so that I would not fall behind. These chaotic years were the ones that shaped me as a lawyer and gave me the skills to become known as one of the go-to DUI attorneys in the state of Connecticut.

In 2000, I left the public defender's office to work alongside the man who inspired me to be a criminal defense attorney – my father. We worked together for one year at Gaston and Ruane, where my father was a partner. In 2001, my father and I decided to set off on our own. We opened Ruane Attorneys, a modest criminal defense firm in Bridgeport. 16 years later, we have two additional locations, another senior partner, 8 associate attorneys, and a dedicated administrative team of 8.

Attorney Teresa DiNardi

I am Attorney Teresa DiNardi, better known around courthouses all over Connecticut as "Lady DUI". I have handled every type of DUI case in Connecticut, from arraignments all the way up to the Connecticut Appellate court and I have been featured in The New York Times for my defense work. Since 2006, I have devoted my practice to the defense of the drinking driver, and developed my reputation and name as "Lady DUI" through my aggressive and educated defense of my clients.

During my three years of law school, I often thought about what type of attorney I would become. It might sound corny, but the truth is that when I entered law school, I did so because I always felt that my life's calling was to help people. I realized very early on that I wanted to be the type of attorney that put people first. I am a fighter, and fighting legal battles for my clients is what I enjoy most.

My clients are underdogs who stand alone against the power of the State of Connecticut to prosecute them with extensive resources. I love standing shoulder-to-shoulder with my clients and doing everything I can to protect and defend them against criminal charges. I passionately believe in our criminal justice system and in the defendable rights granted by the Constitution of the United States.

These values were instilled in me at an early age by my father. During his 27 years as a police officer, he was a hostage negotiator for the Town of Newington, helping many people in difficult and life-threatening situations over the course of his career. The seriousness of his job was expressed to me every day when he would take off his bulletproof vest and place it on the kitchen table for the next day of work. Police officers live by the motto of "To Protect and Serve". I take the same mentality when it comes to my clients. I want nothing less than to get the best possible result for every client.

RUANE ATTORNEYS

Ruane Attorneys has excelled through the experience of our attorneys, the methods that we developed in the years that we have been practicing, and our team's dedication to criminal defense. Even today, as the largest criminal defense firm in Connecticut, we still focus on criminal defense – in particular, DUI defense. This is an essential element of our law practice and an aspect of our firm that we take pride in.

Over the years, we have not been satisfied to sit back and relax. Instead, we dedicate a minimum of 40 hours each year to continuing our education in DUI defense. Jay has completed the rigorous NHTSA Standardized Field Sobriety Testing course and our lawyers are recognized as some of the best DUI defense lawyers in the state. We regularly speak on these topics at various seminars.

This book is a culmination of our experience in DUI defense. However, it is important to note that this book is in no way a replacement for the assistance of a dedicated criminal defense lawyer. The intention of this book is to give you the basic information that you need to understand the DUI process, but we also recommend consulting with a criminal defense lawyer for specific information regarding your situation. We are happy to talk with you about your questions and comments regarding this book as well as your DUI case. Please contact us at 203-925-9201 to talk about your case today.

Chapter 1:
An Introduction to DUI

The purpose of why we are writing this book is to illuminate what happens when you are arrested for DUI in the State of Connecticut. The more familiar you are with the criminal justice system and the related environment, the more you can break down various myths, ease your mind, and focus on what is most important: getting your life back. The best way to benefit from this book is to read it from cover to cover. However, if you need to just get information from a specific chapter, this is acceptable. Reading through this book will give you the perspective necessary to understand the various aspects of your DUI case.

To begin, most of our clients have never been arrested and charged with a crime. Despite the common occurrence of DUI arrests, people accused of driving under the influence are decent, law-abiding citizens who have never been in trouble before. It is key to remember from the outset that DUI is an incredibly complex area of law to understand. Also, the stakes for defendants are high in comparison to other crimes.

Therefore, navigating the criminal justice system is intimidating and you are most likely emotional and deeply concerned about your future. This is perfectly normal given what just happened. Being accused of a crime is a stress-inducing process that terrifies most; it is the recognition of the seriousness of the situation. Your job, home, and family could be at stake. Even the best attorneys walking the face of the Earth get nervous before going to court for trial.

Chapter 2:
Beginning of a DUI Case

When you are arrested for DUI in the State of Connecticut, two separate cases are being brought against you. The first is through the Connecticut Superior Court and involves criminal charges. The second is through the Department of Motor Vehicles and involves your ability to operate a motor vehicle. These cases are largely separate from one another even though both are functions of the state government.

In the State of Connecticut, a DUI case begins with an arrest by a police officer. Before this arrest occurs, you need to understand why the police stopped you in the first place.

REASONABLE SUSPICION

In order to stop a driver in Connecticut, police need what is called "reasonable suspicion". Reasonable suspicion is based on the good faith belief of the police officer that a violation of a law is taking place. Reasonable suspicion gives a police officer the right to briefly detain a person for investigatory purposes. It is important to note that reasonable suspicion requires more than a hunch but less than hard evidence. A series of individual, normal facts can be combined to form the basis for reasonable suspicion. An example would be a person who fits the description of a criminal suspect.

A question many of our clients have is, "Why did the police pull me over?" Many have trouble understanding that reasonable suspicion gives police legal authority to temporarily detain you, but the absence of reasonable suspicion doesn't require officers to tell you that you can leave. Police officers can use their training and experience to ask uncertain people incriminating questions. While legally voluntary, the police will often use nervousness as an opportunity to gather evidence in an attempt to arrest you. I suggest that in situations in which you are interacting with the police, politely ask a police officer, "Am I free to leave?" If the officer doesn't give you a straightforward answer or persists in asking questions, continue to ask, "Officer, am I free to leave?"

Simply refusing to answer an officer's questions does not create reasonable suspicion, but acting nervously and answering questions inconsistently can create reasonable suspicion. Keep in mind that if you are not free to leave, you are being detained. The officer might have some reason to believe you committed a crime and you could be arrested. I recommend that if you are unsure of your answers to any questions, you tell the police that you have decided to remain silent and you would like to see a lawyer.

ARREST

An "arrest" is a seizure of a person by the police based on "probable cause", which is required based upon your Fourth Amendment rights under the Constitution. To establish probable cause, police officers have to be able to show facts that lead them to believe you committed a crime. A police officer can't just say, "I thought he/she was operating a car under the influence." Specific facts must be shown to indicate it is more probable than not that you committed a crime. Only judges, operating under a different branch of government than the police, have the final say in court on whether probable cause existed in your case.

In order to arrest someone for a DUI violation, the police officer must believe that the person in question was operating or in actual physical control of a vehicle and was under the influence of alcohol or another drug. In Connecticut, a police officer has to have probable cause to believe you were driving while impaired by alcohol or drugs in order to request a breath or blood sample. In exploring whether a legal challenge is viable, some questions to think about in relation to your case are:

- When were you told by the police you were under arrest?
- Were you handcuffed by the police?

- What did the police officer tell you about your arrest?
- Did the police officer give you any legal advisements in terms of results?
- Were you told by the police that you have the right to remain silent, and that anything that you tell the police can be used against you in a court of law?
- If yes, and you were informed of your rights, where did this take place?
- Were you advised before taking the breath testing device of the DMV consequences for a refusal?
- Did the officer say anything that made you feel as if you were compelled to submit to a test?
- Did the officer demand that you take a specific test?
- What were the officer's responses to any of your questions?

In regards to the breath testing device, here are some questions that could potentially be important for your case:

- Where were you taken in order to give a breath sample?
- How long were you at the location before taking the breath test?
- Where did you wait prior to taking the breath test?
- Were you continuously observed by the police within 15 minutes prior to taking the breath test?
- Did you have anything in your mouth prior to taking the breath test?
- Were you asked by the police if you had anything in your

mouth prior to taking the breath test?

- Did a police officer look in your mouth before you took the test?
- Did the officer remove anything from your mouth before the test?
- Did the officer ask you to say anything if you burped or belched?
- Did you burp or belch prior to taking the test?
- Did you have an upset stomach prior to taking the test?
- How many people were present when you blew into the machine?
- If there was a refusal, were there two officers present?
- If there was a refusal, did you explicitly tell the police that you refused to take the test?

Some questions relating to your medical history may or may not be relevant, especially questions about the results of the breath testing device test and any performance on field sobriety tests. Some questions to think about are:

- Are you currently seeing a physician, and if so, for what?
- Were you taking any prescription or non-prescription drugs at the time of the arrest?
- Do you have diabetes, and if so, did you tell the police that you do?
- Do you have vision problems?

After the Arrest

After a DUI arrest, the arresting town/city police department or Connecticut State Police gives you a summons and releases you, calling a person capable of driving to pick you up. The summons contains the criminal charges alleged against you as well as the date and time of the first court appearance. The summons is incredibly important, the appearances in court are mandatory and if a court appearance is skipped, you could be charged with the crime of "Failure to Appear".

Some people will have a monetary bond placed on them and will be held in custody until it is paid. Once released on a bond, the court may add conditions to the release. These could potentially include travel restrictions. You cannot violate the conditions of your release of your bond, or you could face more criminal charges.

The arresting police department will also file the charges with the clerk's office at the Superior Court in which your case will be heard. The clerk's office will create and open up a file for your case and assign what is referred to as a "docket number". The court that will handle your appearance will be a Superior Court. The basic timeline for a DUI case can vary; some take just a few weeks, while a few complicated cases may drag out for over a year. Various factors affect the length of this timeline, including whether the case goes to trial.

Initially, your case will appear on the docket, which is a

calendar or list of cases for trial. The "regular" docket is the one in which all new cases are assigned. Your case will likely be maintained on this regular docket for the first few appearances, and may be resolved on this docket. During your court appearances, the State's Attorney and your lawyer will discuss the merits of both the State's case and your defenses; however, these discussions are conducted in private. The main reason for this practice is that any information, when discussed in private, cannot be used in the prosecution of the case. If these discussions were to be conducted in open court, there would be witnesses who could be called on to testify about the case.

If the discussions with the prosecutor and your attorney don't yield a satisfactory disposition, the matter will be set down for judicial pretrial. Most courts have a judge who controls the criminal docket. This judge is known as the presiding judge, who will sit as the final arbiter of the matter before it is determined that the case cannot be resolved without a trial. After a judicial pretrial, the Court will make an offer to resolve the case after hearing from the prosecution and the defense lawyer. Both sides often propose different disposition possibilities and the judge listens to both sides to see what is a reasonable disposition given the legal and factual claims made.

If the State's Attorney, your attorney, and you agree to a satisfactory disposition of the case, you may be required to do certain things. Paying a fine, completing alcohol counseling or complying with probation are all possible conditions. If you plead guilty to a crime, the judge is required to ask you a series of questions in order to determine if you are knowingly and voluntarily pleading to the charges.

There are three ways to plead or be found guilty. The first way is what is referred to as a “straight” guilty plea. A straight plea means you agree with the allegations; the State claims you committed a crime and you agree that you are guilty. The second way to plead guilty is a guilty plea under the Alford Doctrine. The Alford Doctrine means that you don’t agree with some or all of the facts that the State claims happened. However, in light of what you know about the State’s proof, you would like to plead guilty and accept a definite disposition rather than risk going to trial and losing.

The third and final way to plea guilty is to plea “nolo contendere”, which is Latin for “no contest”. This means that you are not contesting the charges nor are you putting up any defenses to the charges. The judge, after hearing the charges, will find you guilty and sentence you. A nolo contendere plea is often used by defendants in situations where they could be sued in civil court like a car accident, for example. A nolo contendere plea cannot be used against a defendant in civil court the way a guilty plea can.

If a case simply cannot be resolved without a trial, both attorneys are then given an opportunity to file motions. Motions are simply requests that are made of the court to grant some type of relief. The relief often requested by defense attorneys is that some part of the State's evidence be excluded from trial. Attorneys may seek to exclude a breath testing device test, a blood test, field sobriety tests, or a statement made by the defendant.

In addition, your attorney might make a motion for the prosecutor to send him or her "discovery" in your case. Discovery is a general legal term that relates to production of evidence that the State intends to present against you in court. An example of discovery would be the list of the State's witnesses against you, plus any information on how to locate them. Obtaining discovery allows your attorney to be as fully prepared as possible when entering the court so that there won't be any surprises. One of the key aspects of discovery may be a videotape of your arrest, either at the scene, in the station, or both.

Most State's Attorneys in Connecticut follow a policy of having open files from the beginning of the case, which allows the defense attorney to view the police report and other evidence in the file. Some only allow a copy of the police report, and others only allow notes to be taken.

The elimination of harmful evidence is the primary purpose and goal of motions. There is not a jury present at the motions hearing, but other people present include the judge, your attorney, the prosecutor, and the State's witness (the police officer who arrested you). The judge will hear each side's arguments, then either grant or deny the motions. However, most judges refuse to hear motions until the day of the trial.

In the timeline of case, a trial follows the motions hearings. The trial can be either a jury trial (a six person jury is commonly used in misdemeanor cases) or a bench trial, which is heard only by a judge. If your case is set down for a trial, you and your attorney will be summoned to begin jury selection, or what is referred to in legal terms as *voir dire*, French for "to speak the truth". The Constitution of the State of Connecticut allows for a defense attorney to question each potential juror independently about their knowledge of the case, the witnesses, and their general outlook on life. During this phase, both the State and your defense attorney are trying to find the best possible candidates who are sympathetic to their side. The prosecutor is looking for candidates who will vote guilty and convict you of the charges, while the defense attorney is trying to find candidates who will vote not guilty.

In Connecticut, there are no long opening statements like the ones seen in television and movie courtroom scenes. In fact, there won't be any opening statements in your case unless the judge has approved them beforehand. The prosecutor will call the first witness for the State, which often is the police officer that arrested you. After the State has asked questions of the first witness, your lawyer will be allowed to cross examine the witness and this process will continue until the State has no more witnesses to call.

According to both federal and state constitutions, the defense doesn't have any burden whatsoever to introduce evidence. If the defense chooses not to introduce evidence, both sides then make their closing arguments.

Chapter 3:
Retaining an Attorney

Law firms handle different areas of law: criminal defense, personal injury, bankruptcy, family law, wills and estate planning, etc. In addition, some attorneys in Connecticut only practice criminal defense including a broad range of cases along with DUI such as white-collar crimes, sexual assaults, and domestic violence. When choosing to hire an attorney for a DUI case, you should ask that attorney what percentage of his or her practice is focused on DUI cases. You should look to hire a DUI defense lawyer who has a large knowledge base regarding the total sphere of laws, procedure, and science that DUI cases encompass. There are many intricacies of DUI law, and even the tiniest detail could potentially affect the outcome of your case and the status of your driver's license. Many attorneys advertise DUI defense. Based on our experience of handling thousands of DUI cases, we recommend hiring an attorney who focuses his or her entire practice on Connecticut DUI law, rather than a general practitioner.

The sooner you consult with and retain an attorney, the better off you will be. The few weeks after the arrest are absolutely critical, and you have to put yourself in the best position to move forward and get a favorable outcome. Also, time-sensitive information (such as a DMV reference number and other documents) need to be passed on to your attorney as soon as possible to prepare for your DMV hearing.

In order to discuss your case with the prosecutor, your attorney will need to know details about your motor vehicle and criminal history. The events leading up to the arrest are also vitally important and your attorney will request your narrative of exactly what happened the day or night of the arrest.

Some of the questions that may be relevant to your case are:

- Where were you the night of your arrest?
- Did you consume any prescription medication within a day of the arrest?
- Did the officer tell you the basis for the traffic stop?
- Who were you with when you were pulled over?
- What did the officer say to you when you were first pulled over?
- Did you admit to drinking alcohol?

If you were stopped at a DUI checkpoint, your attorney

may need to know the following information:

- Did you know that a sobriety checkpoint was ahead?
- Were you given any notice of the checkpoint?
- If so, what type of notice was given?
- Where you given an opportunity ahead of the checkpoint to avoid the checkpoint?
- How many other cars were ahead of you at the checkpoint?
- Did you attempt to turn away from the checkpoint before reaching it?
- How long did you have to wait in line at the checkpoint?
- Did you notice any pattern in which vehicles were being directed into the checkpoint?
- What did the initial conversation with the officer who approached your window consist of?

If you were involved in a car accident in addition to a DUI case, some of the questions involved will be:

- How exactly did the accident occur?
- Did the airbag deploy?
- Were you injured?
- Was any other passenger in your vehicle injured?
- If yes, what were the injuries?
- Was anyone else in another vehicle injured?
- After the accident, did you leave the scene of the

accident?

- Did you call the police or did someone else call?

To determine evidence of sobriety during initial police contact, your attorney may ask these questions:

- How did the officer approach the vehicle?
- What did the officer first say to you?
- Did the officer ask if you had been drinking?
- How did you respond?
- Did the officer ask for license, registration, and proof of insurance?
- If the answer is yes, where were these documents located?
- Did you have any problems locating these documents?
- Did the police officer ask anyone else in the vehicle any other questions?
- If yes, what did they respond?
- Did you have any additional conversation with the officer before getting out of the vehicle?

Questions involving field sobriety tests include:

- Did the officer request that you step out of the vehicle in order to perform field sobriety tests?
- Did the officer inform you that these tests are voluntary?
- Did you agree to perform these tests?

- Did you have any issues whatsoever getting out of the car (i.e. stumbling, tripping, balance, etc.)
- Did the police officer ask if you have any medical conditions that could affect you taking the field sobriety tests?
- If yes, what was your response?
- Do you have any medical issues that could have affected your performance?
- What type of shoes were you wearing?
- Do you wear contact lenses?
- Where specifically did the officer make you perform these tests?
- What were the weather conditions like when you performed these tests?
- Were any emergency lights flashing from the police officer's vehicles when you were performing these tests?

Chapter 4: Court Basics

One of the biggest issues that causes untold stress for our clients is the waiting period. In the majority of criminal cases, your attorney can do absolutely nothing to speed up the waiting process because the control lies with the clerk of the court, judges, and prosecutors. The court system moves at their own pace depending on the amount of cases that are ahead of yours. If your case is delayed for a few months, don't worry. It is because your case has to wait its turn in the regular rotation of the court docket.

There are times when your attorney will intentionally delay your case, which is referred to as a "continuance". These are extended periods to provide accommodation for your case to increase your chances for a better result. Try not to stress during the waiting periods; your attorney is doing what is in your best interest and you have to trust his or her decisions.

Courthouses

In the State of Connecticut, various courts are granted powers by the Connecticut Constitution. A DUI charge is considered a criminal matter, so your case will be called in a Connecticut Superior Court near you. This section of the Superior Court is called a GA, or "geographical area", and encompasses the geographical region of Connecticut appropriate for your case. For example, Hartford Superior Court is known as G.A. 14, which serves the towns of Avon, Bloomfield, Canton, Farmington, Hartford, and West Hartford.

Prosecution and Defense

The person representing the interests of the State of Connecticut is called a State's Attorney. This person is prosecuting you for the DUI charge. If you are familiar with television and movies that deal with legal issues, oftentimes this person is referred to as a DA or District Attorney. In Connecticut, they are referred to as State's Attorneys. The State's role in the criminal justice system is to prosecute a person (the defendant) who is accused of breaking the law. The Defense Attorney represents and defends the Constitutional rights of the defendant in a court of law.

Types of Cases

There are different kinds of criminal cases, depending on

the severity of the offense. Felonies are crimes that are punishable by prison sentences of more than one year while misdemeanors are punishable by prison sentences of one year or less. Other cases include violations, which include motor vehicle cases punishable by a fine only. In addition, infractions may include cases where a fine may be paid by mail without requiring a court appearance (for example, traffic tickets). All are criminal cases but the most serious ones are heard in geographical area courts around the state.

DRESSING FOR COURT

The clothing that a defendant wears is a statement to the judge and an impression on the prosecutor, marshals, and the court staff including the clerk. We always advise our clients to wear business clothing to court. For male clients, this means a suit, dress shoes, tie, etc. A sports jacket and dress shirt are acceptable as well. For female clients, a business suit is preferred; however, a formal dress shirt, blouse or sweater with clean and pressed dress pants is satisfactory. It is not recommended to wear jeans, hats, t-shirts, or any revealing clothing to court. Also, dressing for court is not the time or place to make a fashion statement.

Chapter 5:
People Involved in Your Case

Judges

The judge is the person who presides over the courtroom. The judge will sit at a bench on an elevated platform that stands above the rest of the courtroom. The judge has a large number of responsibilities that take place over the length of a day in court. Fairness is paramount to what a judge does in a courtroom, and the judge has to make sure that proceedings are fair to both the prosecution and the defendant. A judge has to make determinations of admissibility of evidence, which refers to what evidence can or cannot be presented in your case. The judge also has to determine what law applies to each case. If there is a conviction of a defendant, or a defendant pleads guilty to a charge, the judge has to issue a sentence of punishment for the defendant.

Prosecutors

In Connecticut, the State's Attorney's Office is where the

prosecutors work. These attorneys are responsible for prosecuting people accused of crimes in the State of Connecticut. The State's Attorney represents the government and looks to convict on pending charges. Defendants should interact with the prosecutor in court in a polite and respectful manner.

JUDICIAL MARSHALS

In Connecticut, Judicial Marshals are sworn peace officers, whose responsibilities include transporting and processing prisoners, acting as bailiffs and providing judicial and courthouse security. They are stationed at the entrances to all Courthouses in Connecticut and provide mandatory metal detector services.

POLICE OFFICERS

Police officers are the first law enforcement agents involved in an arrest. They are not required to appear in court for pretrial court hearings, but could appear at DMV hearings, motion hearings, or a trial. They often act as witnesses for the prosecution at trial.

LAY WITNESSES

In the context of criminal law, the term "lay witness" is a phrase for a witness who is not an expert, unlike doctors or police officers. In a DUI case, lay witnesses may include any eyewitnesses to a car accident, passengers in the car, complaining parties, or anyone else involved in the case.

LAB TECHNICIANS

If a blood sample is involved in a DUI case, the State's Attorney's Office will likely have one or more lab technicians involved for a potential trial. These scientists do blood testing at forensic laboratories relating to the collection and storage of samples.

EXPERT WITNESSES

In the context of legal jargon, an expert witness is not an eyewitness to the case, but a person who gives an opinion based on advanced knowledge and expertise in a particular area. In order for a party to be considered an expert in a case, the judge has to find that the specific witness is qualified to give an opinion on the subject. A common example of an expert witness is a toxicologist. Experts are expensive, but can add a significant amount of substance to the defense.

COURT CLERKS

A court clerk sits next to the judge and assists in running the courtroom. Clerks are the second-most important person in the room; only judges have more power over courtroom proceedings. Lawyers and clients are encouraged to be respectful and patient with the court clerk and I always make sure to know who the clerk is when I am at court.

Probation Officers

If convicted of an offense, a defendant is placed on probation as part of the sentence and assigned a probation officer. Probation officers work for the court system and make sure the terms and conditions assessed by the court are being followed. If the terms of probation are violated, the probation officer will let the judge and prosecution know what happened. The violator will have to return to court to respond to the allegation.

Investigators

Investigators may be a part of either the defense or prosecution. They basically investigate legal cases, and try to find out information to assist either side in our adversarial-based legal system. Investigators perform such tasks as locating witnesses, serving subpoenas, and finding evidence.

Chapter 6:
Connecticut DUI Laws

Understanding the criminal charges against you is a good way to start breaking down what happens in a DUI case. Connecticut's DUI laws are different from other states', and you need to know specifically what they are and how they will impact your case.

In order to understand what happened when you were arrested, you need to know what the law is. Connecticut DUI law consists of two major statutes: 14-227a and 14-227b. You probably have already seen these on the paperwork you were given by the police after your arrest. The first statute, 14-227a, prohibits a person from driving:

- "Under the influence" of alcohol or drugs, or
- With an "elevated blood alcohol content".

You may have heard terms such as DWI (Driving While Impaired); DUII (Driving Under the Influence of Intoxicants); OUI (Operating Under the Influence) and OWI (Operating While Intoxicated). These terms in Connecticut refer to the 14-227 statute.

For the purposes of the statute, a person is "under the influence" if his or her ability to drive is influenced to a measurable degree. The blood alcohol content (BAC) for each driver in terms of the limit depends upon the age of the driver as well as the type of vehicle driven. An elevated BAC is:

- .08 for drivers over the age of 21.
- .02 for drivers under the age of 21.
- .04 for drivers operating commercial vehicles such as a large truck.

Many of our clients learn about the implications of their behavior in relation to the law after their arrest. According to the case of Infield v. Sullivan, 151 Conn. 506 (1964), a person is "under the influence" if their ability to operate a motor vehicle is affected to an appreciable degree. You can be prosecuted without any evidence of your BAC. Also, DUI law applies to Connecticut drivers operating motor vehicles off-road as well, including snowmobiles and ATVs.

The court's interpretation of intent is unknown to many Connecticut residents and I have seen many clients suffer from this interpretation. In the case of State v. Ducatt, 22 Conn. App. 88, the Appellate court addressed the "keys in the ignition" rule as whether a car is being operated. For the purposes of the DUI statute, having the keys in the ignition meets the legal element of operation. Again, the car doesn't even need to move and the driver doesn't have to give the car gas; simply having the keys in the ignition legally meets the legal test of operation.

The second law, 14-227b, is what is referred to as an "implied consent" law. In Connecticut, licensed drivers consent to be tested for alcohol or drugs when they operate motor vehicles on Connecticut roadways. The law also establishes license suspension procedures by the DMV for drivers who refuse to take a test for drugs or alcohol. This is called an "administrative per se" suspension by the DMV. These DUI laws have specific evidentiary admissibility for alcohol and drug tests and guidelines for criminal penalties and license suspensions.

Criminal punishments include fines, prison time, and license suspensions. By the law of Connecticut, the Department of Motor Vehicles has to impose a 45-day license suspension for those drivers aged 21 and older convicted of DUI. Once re-instated, those convicted can only drive a vehicle with an "ignition interlock device" (IID) for a mandated period of time depending on the total number of prior convictions.

Ignition Interlock Device (IID)

Ignition interlock devices are designed and installed in motor vehicles to stop people from operating a motor vehicle while under the influence of alcohol. The IID requires a driver to breathe into it in order to operate the car, truck, etc. If the IID detects a BAC above .025, the vehicle will not start. An IID also requires a driver to intermittently submit a breath sample after the car has started as part of a "rolling retest". Drivers are responsible for all installation and maintenance costs of the IID installed in their car. They must also pay $100 prior to installation to be used as revenue by the DMV to run the Ignition Interlock Device Program. Drivers have to verify with the DMV that they have had the ignition interlock device installed.

First-time offenders will have ignition interlock-equipped vehicles for one year after their suspension ends. Second-time offenders have to have an ignition interlock device for a period of three years following a suspension. The DUI law adds an additional punishment for second-time offenders to drive in a limited fashion during the first year of the three-year interlock period. Second-time offenders can drive only to:

- Work.
- School.
- A drug or alcohol education program; or,
- An ignition interlock device service center.

Those drivers who are convicted of DUI a third time have their licenses revoked by law. A third-time offender can seek restoration of his or her license after two years. The DMV Commissioner can restore the driver's license on the condition that the driver only drive ignition interlock-equipped vehicles. This condition can be lifted after driving an IID vehicle for 15 years but the driver would have to request a hearing with good cause being shown. The DUI law also requires the use of an ignition interlock device for two years after the one-year license suspension of those convicted of 2nd degree manslaughter or 2nd degree assault with a motor vehicle. These types of crimes apply to drivers who have caused death or serious injury to people while driving under the influence of drugs or alcohol. The court system can order a person arrested for DUI, 2nd degree manslaughter with a motor vehicle, or 2nd degree assault with a motor vehicle to operate vehicles equipped with ignition interlock devices as a condition of:

- Release on bail.
- Probation.
- Granting an application to participate in the Pretrial Alcohol Education Program.

There are penalties for evading ignition interlock restrictions imposed by court order. If a driver asks another person to breathe into an interlock to start a car, or tampers with the device, the driver has committed a class C misdemeanor. This is punishable by up to three months in prison, up to a $500 fine, or possibly both. If a driver operates a motor vehicle that is either not equipped with an interlock device that is functioning, or that a court has prohibited the person from driving, the driver will face stiffer penalties depending upon the offense. These penalties are based upon the number of offenses. The penalty for the first offense is:

- $500-$1,000 fine.
- Up to one year in prison.
- 30 days mandatory minimum jail sentence.

For second offenses:

- $500-$1,000 fine.
- Up to two years in prison.
- 120 days mandatory minimum jail sentence.

For those convicted of a third offense, there is:

- $500-$1,000 fine.
- Up to three years in prison.
- One year mandatory minimum jail sentence.

It should be noted that the court doesn't have to impose the mandatory minimum if there are mitigating circumstances, which must be stated in writing. The DMV has to suspend the driver's license of any nonresident who has committed any of the offenses listed in the previous paragraph for one year. Because many judges are afraid of lobbying groups, they are loath to put mitigating reasons on the record because it could be used against them in future hearings.

A driver is not eligible to operate a motor vehicle with an ignition interlock device if his or her driver's license was suspended for any reason other than a conviction of the following:

- DUI.
- 2nd degree manslaughter with a motor vehicle.
- 2nd degree assault with a motor vehicle.

Implied Consent

Clients often ask what "implied consent" means. Implied consent basically states that anyone who drives on Connecticut's roads implicitly allows the testing of blood, breath, or urine. If the driver is a minor, the parent(s) or legal guardian are technically considered to have given consent. Before administering a chemical test for blood, breath, or urine, a police officer must:

- Inform the driver of his or her constitutional rights.
- Give the driver an opportunity to call a lawyer.
- Inform the driver that his or her license will eventually be suspended if he or she refuses to take the test.
- Inform the driver that evidence of a refusal may be used against them in a criminal prosecution.

The administrative per se law requires license suspension procedures for drivers who refuse to submit to a chemical test or have a result that indicates an elevated BAC above the legal limit. In these types of cases, the police act on behalf of the DMV, and revoke the driver's license for 24 hours and submit a report of what happened to the DMV. The report has to include any test results and the basis for why the officer made the arrest. If there is a test refusal, a third party who witnessed the refusal, often a police officer, must sign the report.

Blood Alcohol Content (BAC) Testing

The DESPP Commissioner has to determine the reliability of the various methods used to test blood, breath, and urine, and certify those used within the State of Connecticut. The Commissioner has to adopt regulations that govern the conduct of tests, the operation and use of the devices, and the training and certification of test operators. The DESPP Commissioner also regulates the drawing of blood, breath, or urine samples. Any evidence that a driver refused to submit to a test is admissible if the procedural requirements of the statute are met. At trial, the court must instruct the jury on what inferences it can or cannot make based on a refusal.

It should be noted that a different set of admissibility standards apply to blood and urine samples taken from a driver during the course of medical treatment. Results from the chemical analysis of the blood and/or urine samples are considered evidence to establish probable cause for the driver's arrest by warrant and are admissible in a prosecution if:

- The sample was taken for the diagnosis and treatment of an injury.
- A blood sample taken was within the DESPP guidelines.

- A police officer satisfies a Superior Court judge that the officer had reason to believe that the driver was operating under the influence of alcohol or drugs, and
- The blood or urine sample constitutes evidence of this offense.
- The judge issues a search warrant authorizing the seizure of test results and possibly the additional seizure of hospital medical records prepared along with the diagnosis and treatment of the injury.

It is not common knowledge, other than to attorneys, that blood drawn at hospitals will come into evidence against a defendant. Many times our clients don't understand that when blood is drawn, it can later be used as evidence for an arrest warrant for DUI, even months after the initial incident. Sometimes, however, problems arise with the identification of the person who drew the defendant's blood.

Police officers can determine a motorist's BAC levels by testing the blood, breath, or urine. The police are allowed to choose the type of test given. The law establishes a presumption that a driver's BAC at the time tested is the same as when he or she was stopped by the police. The law requires two tests at least 10 minutes apart.

Procedurally, a different set of standards apply when someone gives either a blood or urine sample at a police officer's request because these tests require being sent out to a laboratory for analysis. As a result of this requirement, the police officer cannot immediately take possession of the driver's license or follow elements of the per se law. If test results are received showing a BAC over the legal limit, the officer immediately notifies the DMV and submits the required paperwork.

For 16 and 17-year-old drivers, the law imposes a stricter limit of .02 BAC level. A police officer, acting on behalf of the DMV, has the authority to tow the vehicle and seize the driver's license, which is technically suspended for 48 hours beginning at the time of arrest or issued summons. In order to get the license back, a parent or legal guardian of the driver (unless emancipated from his or her parents) has to:

- Appear in person at the police station or state police barracks.
- Sign a document acknowledging the return of the license.

There should not be a restoration fee charged for the return of the driver's license. The officer who acted on behalf of the DMV who seized the license must send a report to the DMV Commissioner. Also, any driver under the age of 18 who is arrested and charged with DUI cannot apply for "Youthful Offender " (YO) status, in which first offenders are prevented from being tried as adults.

LICENSE SUSPENSION

The next steps are based upon the DMV receiving the police report and the driver's factual circumstances. The Commissioner may suspend the driver's license within thirty days from notice of the arrest as long as the driver has not:

- Been previously suspended for a DUI conviction within the past 10 years preceding the current arrest, or
- Been involved in a car accident involved in a fatality.

In the case of a person who has a prior DUI driver's license suspension or has been involved in a fatal accident, the commissioner may suspend the ability to drive on any date, including immediately. Regardless of what happens, a driver is entitled to an administrative hearing before the DMV. If there is no prior DUI suspension or involvement in a fatal accident, the hearing has to take place before the suspension goes into effect. When the DMV does send the documentation, it is important that the driver contact the DMV no later than seven days after the DMV mails the suspension notice. If there is a prior DUI related suspension or a fatal accident, the DMV hearing can occur after the suspension, but not more than thirty days after the person contacts the DMV to schedule the hearing.

The issues to be decided at the DMV hearing are the following:

- Did the police officer have probable cause to make the arrest?
- Was the driver arrested?
- Was he or she driving?
- Did the driver refuse the test or have an elevated BAC?

In the case when test results obtained from a blood sample are taken from a driver who is apparently injured, an additional issue is decided at the hearing. The hearing has to determine whether the test results obtained are competent as evidence. If the answer to any of the previous questions listed above is 'no', the DMV has to return the license to the driver. If the answer to all of the questions is 'yes', the driver's license is suspended for 45 days, and the driver must have an IID installed in his or her car pursuant to these variables:

- 1st offense
    - If over 21 and blow over .08: 6 months IID
    - If under 21 and blow over .02: 1 year IID
    - If test was refused: 1 year IID
- 2nd offense
    - If over 21 and blow over .08: 1 year IID
    - If under 21 and blow over .02: 2 years IID
    - If test was refused: 2 years IID
- 3rd or subsequent offense
    - If over 21 and blow over .08: 2 years IID

- If under 21 and blow over .02: 3 years IID
- If test was refused: 3 years IID

The test refusal penalties also apply to a person who takes the initial breath testing device but refuses to take a second test. The penalties listed above don't apply to someone whose physical condition makes such tests medically inadvisable. These administrative license suspension penalties act in addition to any suspension penalties imposed because of a conviction on criminal DUI charges.

Commercial Driver's License holders who commit two or more of certain motor vehicle offenses, including DUI, are disqualified for life from driving a commercial motor vehicle. Connecticut law now requires that in order to be eligible for reinstatement of their license, disqualified CDL holders have to voluntarily enroll in, and successfully complete the following:

- A substance abuse treatment program established and operated by the Department of Mental Health and Addiction Services (DMHAS).
- A program operated through a licensed substance abuse treatment facility, or
- An equivalent program offered in another state.

As was the law prior, CDL holders have to wait 10 full calendar years for reinstatement.

A driver with a suspended license is subject to a fine between $500 and $1,000 and imprisonment of up to one year if his or her license was suspended for:

- DUI.
- 2nd degree manslaughter with a motor vehicle.
- 2nd degree assault with a motor vehicle.
- Refusing to submit to a BAC test, or
- A BAC test that is elevated above the legal limit.

Also, the offense of operating under suspension carries a 30-day mandatory minimum jail term unless there are mitigating circumstances. A driver who operates a motor vehicle while the driver's license is suspended for a second violation of operating under suspension is subject to:

- $500 to $1,000 fine.
- Imprisonment for up to two years.
- 120 days of which cannot be suspended unless the court specifies mitigating circumstances.

Any driver who operates a motor vehicle while his or her license is suspended for a third time for operating under suspension is subject to:

- $500 to $1,000 fine.
- Imprisonment for up to three years.
- One year of which cannot be suspended unless the court

specifies mitigating circumstances.

The judge has to specify whatever mitigating circumstances, or lack of, in writing.

By Connecticut law, any driver who has had a driver's license suspended, with special exceptions, can apply for a driving permit that allows certain work or education related driving during the suspension period.

PENALTIES

Penalties for a person convicted of DUI are assessed within a timetable that relates back 10 years prior. Any criminal conviction that occurs in another state with DUI laws similar to Connecticut constitutes a prior conviction of the same offense and becomes part of the offender's prior criminal history. In practice, the first DUI conviction for a driver is frequently the driver's second time being arrested and charged. This occurs because the first time someone is arrested for DUI, he or she can apply to the court for admission to the Pretrial Alcohol Education Program. Connecticut law provides for a diversionary Pretrial Alcohol Education Program in which certain defendants charged with DUI can complete alcohol education classes or a substance abuse treatment program. The applicant has to state under oath in court that he or she has never been in the program in the previous 10 years; or, not at all if under the age of 21. The court has to dismiss the charge of DUI if the applicant successfully completes the program.

The criminal penalties for a first conviction of DUI are as follows:

- Up to six months of prison with a mandatory minimum of two days or up to six months suspended with probation requiring 100 hours of community service.
- $500 to $1,000 fine.
- License suspension of 45 days, followed by one year of driving ignition interlock device vehicle.

The second conviction results in:

- Up to two years in prison, with a mandatory minimum of 120 days and probation with 100 hours of community service.
- $1,000 to $4,000 fine.
- License suspension of 45 days, followed by three years of driving IID vehicle.
- Limitations of driving the first year: work, school, an alcohol or drug abuse treatment program or ignition interlock service center.

The third or subsequent conviction results in:

- Up to three years in prison, with a mandatory minimum

of one year in prison and probation with 100 hours of community service.

- $2,000 to $8,000 fine.
- A permanent revocation of driver's license, although you may petition for the restoration of your license after two years.

For second, third, or subsequent DUI convictions, Connecticut law forces an offender to:

- Submit to drug or alcohol assessment through the Judicial Branch Court Support Services Division, and
- Undergo a treatment program, if ordered to do so by the court.

Third-time offenders have their driver's licenses revoked by the DMV. However, after two years, drivers can request that their license be restored. The DMV commissioner can restore the license if it is determined that there is not a danger to public safety, and the driver has met some requirements, including completing an alcohol and drug education program. The driver can only operate vehicles that are equipped with an interlock device. Also, the DUI law places any driver who does not install and use the device as required under a license suspension. This suspension cannot be for a period greater than the period of the original suspension.

Drivers who are convicted of 2nd degree manslaughter

with a motor vehicle or 2nd degree assault with a motor vehicle are to operate vehicles equipped with an IID for two years following a mandatory one-year license suspension. Courts can also order a defendant convicted of either crime to drive motor vehicles that are equipped with an IID as a condition of:

- Release on bail.
- Probation.
- Granting an application to participate in the pretrial Alcohol Education Program.

Drivers who are convicted of operating under the influence with a passenger under 18 in the vehicle face enhanced criminal penalties. The first offense results in:

- Up to one year in prison, with a mandatory minimum of thirty days in prison.
- A fine of $500-$2000.
- Probation with 100 hours community service.
- License suspension of 45 days, followed by an IID period of one year.

The second conviction results in:

- Up to three years in prison, with a mandatory minimum of 180 days in prison.
- A fine of $1000-$4000.
- Probation with 100 hours community service.

- License suspension of 45 days, followed by an IID period of three years with travel restrictions.

The third or subsequent conviction results in:

- Up to five years in prison, with a mandatory minimum of two years in prison.
- A fine of $2000-$8000.
- Probation with 100 hours community service.
- Permanent license suspension.

Drivers who are convicted of operating a school bus or school transportation vehicle while under the influence face the following criminal penalties:

- Between one and ten years in prison. The mandatory minimum is 30 days in prison; however, if there was at least one passenger under the age of 18 in the vehicle, the mandatory minimum is 120 days in prison.
- A fine of up to $10,000.
- Probation with 100 hours community service.
- License suspension of 45 days, followed by an IID period of three years with travel restrictions.

A driver who holds a commercial driver's license (CDL) faces disqualification from driving a commercial motor vehicle for one year if he or she has:

- A BAC of .04 or more while driving a commercial vehicle.
- A BAC of .08 or more while driving any other type of vehicle.
- Refused a BAC test when driving any motor vehicle, or
- Been convicted of DUI.

CDL holders face a lifetime ban on operating commercial motor vehicles by committing certain offenses such as DUI although they can get reinstated if they meet certain conditions. If a driver arrested for DUI operates a vehicle with a suspended license, police can impound the vehicle for 48 hours. The owner of the vehicle can re-claim it after paying the costs of both towing and storage. Also, in addition, people found to be persistent felony offenders of driving under the influence are subject to an increased criminal penalty.

The admissibility of evidence for uninsured drivers is dependent upon whether the driver was injured. In order for the results of a test to be admissible, the following must occur:

- The driver must have been given a reasonable opportunity to call a lawyer before taking the test and consenting to it.
- A copy of the test results have to be mailed or delivered to the driver within 24 hours or the next business day after results are known.
- The test has to be given by a police officer or at the

officer's discretion.

- The test has to be administered using methods and equipment approved by the Department of Emergency Services and Public Protection (DESPP).
- The test equipment has to be checked for accuracy according to DESPP regulations.
- A second test of the same kind has to be administered at least 10 minutes after the first test is conducted unless the second test is to detect drugs; in which case, it can be of a different type and doesn't have to be administered within that time frame.
- The test has to start within two hours of vehicular operation, which is generally the time of the alleged offense.

The DUI law allows the Department of Correction Commissioner to release an inmate that has been sentenced for DUI to what is known as "home confinement". First, the inmate needs to be admitted and conducted a risk and needs assessment to the inmate's home. The inmate that is released cannot leave his or her home without authorization, remaining in DOC custody and under the supervision of DOC employees. The DOC Commissioner can take away the home confinement and force the inmate to go back to prison for violating the release conditions.

Courts in Connecticut may also impose more severe penalties for those considered persistent DUI offenders. A driver is considered a persistent DUI offender if he or she:

- Is convicted of 2nd degree manslaughter with a motor vehicle.
- Is convicted of 2nd degree assault with a motor vehicle, and
- Within the past ten years, has been convicted of either of these charges, DUI, or a similar offense in another state.

Courts can impose a prison sentence for the next higher degree of a charge for a persistent DUI offender. Therefore, the maximum possible prison term for a persistent offender convicted of 2nd degree manslaughter increases from 10 years to 20 years. Also, the punishment for 2nd degree assault with a motor vehicle increases from five years to 10 years.

One question our clients have for us is this: "What about out-of-state DUIs?" By Connecticut law, DUIs and other alcohol related criminal offenses that happened out-of-state are judged by the essential elements of the crime. If the court finds that the essential elements of the out-of-state offense are determined to be substantially similar as Connecticut offenses, this could constitute a prior offense for determining the enforcement of penalties for second or subsequent offenses. According to both federal and state law, states must document convictions for types of highway-related offenses, including DUI. The states have to document these violations if committed by a nonresident so that the home state of the resident can penalize the driver. So, if a person has a prior Connecticut DUI conviction and is subsequently convicted of DUI in another state, the Connecticut DMV knows about the out-of-state conviction and will impose the penalty Connecticut law requires.

Connecticut DMV Process

When you are arrested for DUI in the State of Connecticut, the arresting agency (usually either the State Police or a Town/City Police Department) must report the arrest to the Department of Motor Vehicles. The DMV will process your information and will receive a copy of the police report from the arresting agency. They will then send you a notice by mail letting you know that they are suspending your license, usually within 30 days from the date of the arrest. The reason the DMV is allowed to do this is because of the State's implied consent law that states that whenever you drive on the roads in the State of Connecticut, you have given your consent to submit to a chemical test of your blood, breath, or urine. If you fail this test, or refuse to give a sample, the DMV can strip you of your privilege to drive for a specified time period.

When the DMV issues an automatic administrative per se license suspension, a Per Se hearing is an opportunity to try to save your driver's license from further suspension. The Per Se hearings are held based on four issues:

- Did the police officer have probable cause to arrest the person for operating a motor vehicle while under the influence of intoxicating liquor or drugs or both?
- Was the person placed under arrest?
- Did the person refuse to submit to a test or analysis, or did the person submit to a test within two hours of the time of vehicular with BAC results of .08 or higher?
- Was the person operating the motor vehicle?

BURDEN OF PROOF

In a criminal case, the standard burden of proof is beyond a reasonable doubt. However, in an administrative hearing, the burden is much lower. The State of Connecticut simply has to prove the elements of the offense to be more likely true than not true, referred to as a "preponderance of the evidence". The burden is on you, as the plaintiff at an administrative hearing, to prove that the decision by the DMV to suspend your license is clearly erroneous based upon the evidence. There must be substantial evidence in the record to support the DMV Commissioner's findings.

The reason why the State of Connecticut can do this is because driving is a privilege, not a Constitutional right, and the State can rescind this privilege. What this means is that you, as the respondent, are responsible for providing enough evidence to counter the State's reports beyond a preponderance of the evidence. Many of our clients will ask us if the State's action to suspend their license in addition to pursuing jail time amounts to double jeopardy. The answer, for now, is no. Over 20 years ago, a number of citizens throughout the United States believed this to be true, and a woman named Wendy Hickam appealed her case based upon this issue after she lost her license. The Court ruled that driving is not a constitutional right protected by either the State or Federal Constitution. The Court held that because a driver's license is a privilege and not a Constitutional right, taking it away does not constitute double jeopardy. The reasoning of the judges was based upon the idea that the State of Connecticut has a compelling interest to keep drunk drivers off of the roadways.

There are defenses to the DMV process, however, and if you do not fight the DMV suspension, you will automatically lose because the suspension will go through. During the Per Se hearings, there often are issues like the legitimacy of a refusal of a breath testing device test and the time window of the test in relation to the operation of the motor vehicle. One of the ways a DUI attorney can try to restore your driver's license is to bring in the arresting police officers for cross-examination. The decision to subpoena an officer to a hearing is not one to be taken lightly, especially when the officer's testimony could jeopardize possible defenses to the criminal portion of your case. Only an experienced DUI attorney who has a better sense of the outcome of the decision is qualified to make that determination.

Chapter 7:
Alcohol

Alcohol is an organic compound; it is best described scientifically as comprised of naturally occurring elements with carbon atoms. Alcohol is an intoxicating substance that produces effects when ingested into the human body. There are various types of alcohol, but what we deal with in our job as defense attorneys is ethanol. Ethanol is molecularly described as H3C2-OH. The OH group at the end of the group of molecules is what makes the compound an alcohol.

Ethanol is beverage alcohol, which is the primary ingredient in beer, wine, liquor, etc. The process of alcohol production starts with fermentation, which is a type of decomposition in which the sugars in fruit, grains, etc. combine with yeast to produce ethanol. Ethanol can also be created through the distillation process. Distilled spirits include rum, whiskey, gin, vodka, etc. The alcohol concentration of distilled spirits varies - a can of beer, a glass of wine, and a shot of liquor are roughly the same in terms of alcohol content.

Alcohol is a central nervous system depressant. Alcohol enters into a person's central nervous system (the brain, brain stem, and spinal cord) when a person drinks it. The first step towards absorption is the stomach and the movement of alcohol into the blood. It should be noted, however, that alcohol doesn't have to be digested in order to pass from the stomach to the blood. It can pass directly through the walls of the stomach. Under the right circumstances, absorption of alcohol can take place very quickly.

When alcohol enters into an empty stomach, roughly 80 percent will go through the base of the stomach and end up in the small intestine, where it will be absorbed into the blood. The human body doesn't need to digest the alcohol before allowing it into the bloodstream; the small intestine will be ready to take the alcohol as soon as it hits the stomach.

The intake of food does come into play in DUI cases. Food has to be at least partially digested before it passes into the small intestine. When the brain perceives food to be in the stomach, it tells a muscle located at the base of the stomach to constrict, and it then cuts off the passage to the small intestine. This muscle is known medically as the pylorus, or pyloric valve. As long as it remains constricted, very little will move out of the stomach to the small intestine. If any alcohol is located in the stomach along with food, the alcohol will be trapped behind the pylorus. Some of the alcohol that remains trapped in the stomach will begin to chemically break down before it ever gets into the bloodstream. Over time, the digestive process continues, the pylorus eventually will relax, and some of the alcohol and food will pass through; however, the effect of the stress of the arrest is to slow the absorption significantly. Here is where the human body can work against the DUI driver. When a person is pulled over, the experience is stressful on the mind and body. When a person experiences stress, the body goes into a state of preparation for "flight or fight". When the body does this, it shuts down other immediately unnecessary bodily functions, and since digestion takes a large amount of energy to occur, the digestive system shuts down quickly. When this happens, the body stops processing the contents of the driver's stomach, and 2 things happen. First, a buildup of ethanol vapor will enter the airway and come out when a person talks, causing an officer to smell more alcohol. Secondly, the alcohol won't get processed at that time. Eventually, when the driver is brought to the station, and finally relaxes from the state of stress, the body then reopens that value and floods the system with the contents of the stomach to replace that energy burned off in the stressful state. What happens then? The ethanol hits the bloodstream hardest around the time the breath or blood test is given and the measurement likely doesn't match what was in the breath or blood at the time of driving, but the police and prosecution do not care about this likelihood. Alcohol normally gets into the blood slowly, and the body will continue to process and eliminate the alcohol that manages to get in. The BAC (Blood Alcohol Concentration) of a drinker rises faster if he or she is drinking alcohol on an empty stomach.

Once alcohol moves from the stomach into the bloodstream, it gets distributed throughout the body by the movement and flow of the blood. Alcohol, chemically speaking, has an affinity for water. The bloodstream will carry the alcohol to all of the various tissues and organs of the human body, and eventually will deposit the alcohol into these areas in proportion to their water contents. Brain tissue, for instance, has very high water content, so the human brain receives a substantial share of the distributed alcohol. Muscle tissue also has a reasonably high content of water; therefore, very little alcohol will eventually be deposited in the body fat of a person drinking alcohol. This is different from drugs like PCP and THC, which are fat-soluble.

The natural chemical affinity of alcohol for water, and its lack of affinity for fat, does help explain why alcohol affects men and women differently. The typical female body contains a good deal less water than that of the typical man. This is because women have extra fatty tissue, designed to protect a child during biological development. Scientists have determined that the average male body is about 68 percent water, while the typical female is about 55 percent. Therefore, when a woman drinks, she has less fluid, pound for pound, to receive the distribution of the alcohol. For example, if a woman and a man who weigh exactly the same drink exactly the same amount of alcohol under similar circumstances, the woman's BAC could rise faster than the BAC of the man. Add to this the biological fact that the average woman is smaller than the average man; it becomes obvious that an amount of alcohol will cause a higher BAC in a female than in a male.

As soon as alcohol enters into the bloodstream, the human body starts trying to get rid of it. Some of the alcohol will be removed directly from the body in the same chemical state, basically unchanged. Examples of this would be alcohol exiting the body in the form of breath, urine, sweat, tears, etc. However, only a small portion of the ingested alcohol will be eliminated directly. Most of the alcohol ingested is eliminated by metabolic activity. Metabolism is the process of chemical change. In the case of alcohol, it reacts with oxygen in the body and change, through a series of intermediate steps into both carbon dioxide and water, both of which get directly expelled by the body.

Most metabolic activity of alcohol in the body takes place in the liver. Enzymes act as catalysts to speed up the reaction of alcohol with oxygen. The speed of the reaction varies somewhat from person to person, and even for any given individual at specific times. On average, a person's blood alcohol concentration (BAC) will drop by about .015 per hour after peaking. For example, a person who had a peak BAC level of .15

will take about ten hours to eliminate all of the alcohol.

For the average male, a BAC of .015 is about two-thirds of the alcohol content of the standard drink (a can of beer, a glass of wine, or a shot of alcohol). For the average female, the same BAC would be obtained on just one-half of a standard drink. Essentially, the typical male would eliminate about two-thirds of a drink per hour, while the typical female would only eliminate about half of a drink per hour.

People can control the rate in which alcohol enters into the bloodstream; for example, a person could sip rather than gulp down drinks. A person can drink on an empty stomach, or eat before consuming alcohol. Also, the amount of alcohol to be consumed can be changed - a person can drink a lot or a little. However, once alcohol gets into the blood, there isn't much that can be done to affect the rate in which it leaves the body. A person simply has to wait for the biochemical process of metabolism to move along and rid the body of alcohol.

As a result of people knowing what we do for a living, people often ask us questions such as, "How much can I drink before becoming impaired?" There isn't a simple answer to this question. We know from experience that any amount of alcohol can impact a person's ability to operate a motor vehicle. The laws of nearly every state explicitly establish a BAC limit above which it is unlawful to operate a motor vehicle. However, many states also make it unlawful to drive when "under the influence" of alcohol. So, we often get asked, "How much alcohol does a person have to drink to reach these kinds of BAC levels?" Based on what we have explained so far, it obviously depends. Factors such as the amount of time spent drinking; the person's gender, size and weight; the contents of the person's stomach, etc. all matter.

Hypothetically speaking, a 175-lb male who has two beers in a short time period will have a BAC that should be slightly over .04; two more beers will send the BAC over .08. Connecticut's legal limit for operating a motor vehicle is .08. In this respect, it doesn't take much alcohol to impair a person legally. A couple of beers at the bar with friends can easily do it.

Chapter 8:
Police Detection

Police officers are trained to break DUI stops into three separate phases: Phase One - Vehicle in Motion; Phase Two - Personal Contact; and Phase Three - Pre-arrest Screening. The first phase is based upon observation of the vehicle's movement and the officer's attempt to observer the driver. The second phase gives the police officer time to observe and speak with the driver face-to-face. The third phase is the administration of field sobriety tests. DUI detection doesn't always include all three phases; sometimes there are cases in which one phase is absent because of issues like a car accident or when a driver refuses to submit to field sobriety tests.

Phase One: Vehicle in Motion

In phase one, the police officer has to make a decision based on visual observation whether or not there is sufficient reason to stop a driver. Police are looking for unusual driving such as weaving or very slow speed, or something like a burnt out tail light. During this phase, the officer has to determine if there is sufficient evidence to legally grant reasonable suspicion necessary to carry onward to the next step in DUI detection process. The officer must determine:

- What is the vehicle doing?
- Do I have grounds to stop the vehicle?
- If I give a signal to stop, how does the driver respond?
- How does the driver react when pulled over?

During the first phase of police DUI detection of observing a driver, the police officer has to make one of three choices:

1) Stop the car.
2) Continue to observe.
3) Disregard the car.

Drivers who operate under the influence tend to exhibit symptoms of slowed reactions, impaired judgment, impaired vision and poor coordination. An impaired driver will exhibit visual clues because of the following complexities of operating a motor vehicle:

- Steering the car.
- Pressing the accelerator.
- Using turn signals.

- Pressing the brake.
- Observing traffic.
- Watching signal lights, stop signs, etc.
- Making decisions about where to turn.

Police look for additional visual clues of impairments such as:

- Weaving – car movement toward one side of the roadway and then quickly toward the other side, like a zigzag movement.
- Weaving across lane lines – extreme cases of weaving in which the vehicle's wheels move across lane lines before the driver corrects his/her path.
- Straddling lane line – the vehicle is moving straight ahead with the center lane in between both the left and right wheels of the car.
- Swerving – a jarring turn away from a straight course.
- Turning with a wide radius – a much wider turn than normal in terms of the center of the turn being much greater than normal.
- Drifting – a straight-line movement of a car at a slight angle in relation to the road.
- Almost striking an object or vehicle.

Speeding and braking problems also can be taken into

consideration. Some of these include:

- Stopping issues – stopping with a jerking motion, stopping abruptly, stopping too far from a curb, and stopping either too short or beyond a stop bar at an intersection.
- Accelerating or decelerating rapidly – any driving that is either too fast or too slow in relation to driving conditions.
- Varying speed – alternating between speeding up and slowing down.
- Very slow speed – a vehicle that is being driven less than 10 mph than posted limit.

Vigilance issues include:

- Driving in an opposite lane or the wrong way on a one-way street – a vehicle that is going into an opposing lane, not yielding the right of way, driving the wrong way, etc.
- Slow response to traffic signals – the observed vehicle exhibits a response to a traffic signal that is delayed; for example, a driver that is not responding to a green light.
- Slow or failing to respond to a police officer's signals – driver is very slow to react to an officer's hand signals, lights, or sirens.
- Stopping in a lane for no reason – no justifiable reason for the vehicle to stop in the traffic lane.

Phase Two: Personal Contact

During the second part of the DUI screening process, police officers approach and observe the driver still in the vehicle to note any indications of impairment. During the face-to-face interaction, the police officer tries to determine if the driver is impaired. Based upon the up close observation of the driver, combined with previous observations of the car in motion, the police officer determines if there is legitimate reason to tell the driver to exit the vehicle.

The face-to-face observations and interview of the driver by a police officer is based upon the senses of sight, hearing, and smell. In terms of sight, there are a variety of things that a police officer is looking for to determine alcohol and/or drug use including:

- Bloodshot eyes.
- Dirty clothes.
- Fumbling of hands/fingers.
- Containers of alcohol.
- Drugs or drug paraphernalia.
- Unusual actions.

In terms of hearing, the police officer listens for:

- Slurring of speech.
- Any admission of drinking.

- Abusive language.
- Unusual statements.
- Responses that are inconsistent.

In terms of smell, the police officer notices:

- Smell of alcohol.
- Smell of marijuana.
- Air freshener scents.
- Breath sprays/mouthwash.
- Unusual odors.

A technique that police officers use in terms of establishing evidence of alcohol intoxication is the concept of "divided attention". These tasks require the driver to focus on two or more things at the same time. Some of the techniques used are asking for two things at the same time, asking interrupting questions, and asking unusual questions. One of these techniques is to ask for both the driver's license and the vehicle registration at the same time. Police officers are trained to look for drivers who:

- Forget to produce both documents.
- Produce documents other than those requested.
- Fail to see license, registration or both while looking through wallet or purse.
- Drops or fumble through wallet, purse, etc.

- Cannot retrieve documents using fingertips.

When police officers ask interrupting or distracting questions, it forces the driver to divide attention between searching for a driver's license and answering a new question. Police officers are trained to look for drivers that:

- Ignore the question and concentrate on the license and registration search.
- Forget to keep searching after answering the question asked by police.
- Supply an incorrect answer to the question.

Police use the technique of asking unusual questions after gaining possession of your driver's license and registration. An example would be a police officer asking you your middle name. These types of questions require a driver to process information, which can be difficult when a driver doesn't expect to have to answer them. Another technique used is having a driver recite part of the alphabet. Police officers will often instruct a driver to begin with a letter other than the letter A and stop at a letter other than the letter Z. An example would be asking a driver to begin with the letter G and ending with the letter W.

Another technique is to require the subject to count multiple numbers in reverse. For example, counting backwards from the number 88 to the number 53. This task divides the attention of a driver because the driver has to continue to concentrate throughout the whole process.

If a police officer does instruct you to exit the vehicle, this decision is made if the officer suspects that you are impaired. When a driver steps out of and walks away from a vehicle, a police officer is looking for the following behavior:

- Shows anger towards an officer.
- Can't follow instructions.
- Can't open the door.
- Leaves the car in gear.
- Climbs out slowly.
- Leans against the car.
- Keeps hands on the car for balance.

Remember, the police are trying to find sensory evidence of alcohol/drug influence to make a DUI arrest.

Police officers that are successful in DUI stops have the ability to recognize the sense-based evidence of alcohol and/or other drugs, and have the ability to describe that evidence clearly in a police report. For accurate DUI enforcement, police officers train to use detection to collect evidence and graphically describe their observations in a police report. Through a police report, a police officer communicates with many different parties in a DUI case. Some of these parties include superior officers such as a lieutenant or sergeant, the prosecutor, judge, jury, and defense attorneys.

Phase Three: Pre-Arrest Screening

After probable cause is found by a police officer, an officer will oftentimes try to recover more evidence that the driver is under the influence of alcohol. At this time, the officer might ask the driver to perform Field Sobriety Tests. These tests are not required in every state although consent to a blood, breath, or urine test varies depending upon the state. These tests, which are usually conducted on the side of the road, do nothing to prove a person's sobriety, and often hurt the driver's case. The police cannot force a driver to perform these tests, so the driver should politely decline to take them.

Chapter 9:
Field Sobriety Tests

In order to establish the basis for a DUI arrest, the officer will often administer three field sobriety tests. Standardized Field Sobriety Tests (SFST) are best described as psychophysical tests. These tests are considered by some to be an objective and standardized measure of a sample of behavior. They focus on three elements:

- Objectivity: aspects of a test are based on objective criteria, such as the scoring or the interpretation of the score, and are not influenced by the subjective opinion of the examiner.
- Standardization: a uniformity of procedure in the administration, scoring, and interpretation of the test and its results.
- Behavior Sample: a representative sample of a person's behavior from which one can draw inferences and hypotheses.

It should be noted that tests like the Field Sobriety Tests

are not a mental x-ray; they do not reveal hidden mental states of mind. To be valid, psychological tests have to meet three types of criteria:

- Reliability.
- Standardization.
- Validity.

These types of psychological tests are used by a wide variety of professionals, including psychologists, special education teachers, guidance counselors, psychiatrists, nurses, engineers, etc. Ideally, psychophysical tests should require an evaluation of a person's appearance, condition, and ability to follow instruction. Also, issues such as balance and coordination should be included. These are known as divided attention tests, because they require the subject to focus on more than one thing at a time. Scientific studies have shown that a person under the influence of alcoholic beverages may be able to perform one test, but rarely two.

The National Highway Traffic Safety Administration (NHTSA), with cooperation and assistance from the law enforcement community, conducted extensive research that ultimately produced a battery of three standardized tests:

1. Horizontal gaze nystagmus.
2. Walk-and-turn.
3. One-leg-stand.

These tests are used by police officers in detecting impaired drivers.

The origins of this program lie in laboratory and field studies conducted by the Southern California Research Institute; the tests were originally developed by the LAPD. In 1986, the Advisory Committee on Highway Safety of the International Association of Chiefs of Police (IACP) passed a resolution that recommended law enforcement agencies adopt and implement the field sobriety testing developed by the NHTSA. As the program developed over time, it became apparent that nationally accepted standards should be enacted.

Horizontal Gaze Nystagmus

In Connecticut, the first test often given is what is known as the "horizontal gaze nystagmus" (HGN) test. Nystagmus sounds like a complicated word but it just means an involuntary jerking of the eyes. Also, the person experiencing the nystagmus is not aware that the jerking is occurring. The HGN test is based upon the idea that involuntary jerking of the eyes becomes noticeable when a person is impaired by alcohol. The theory is that the higher the blood alcohol concentration goes, the sooner the eyes will jerk as they move to the side of the person's head. Many police officers consider the HGN test to be the most reliable test. Before giving the HGN test, police will look for signs of possible medical impairment including pupil size, resting nystagmus, and tracking ability.

When administering the HGN test, police officers usually have the person follow the motion of a small pen with the eyes only, nothing else. The tip of something that contrasts with the background is used as the stimulus. When administered, the police start with the left eye, looking for three specific clues. As the eye moves from side to side, the officer is checking to see if the eye moves smoothly or whether it jerks noticeably. The theory is based on the idea that as people become more impaired by alcohol, the eyes show a lack of smooth pursuit as they move from side to side. When the eyes move as far to one side as possible, the police officer is trying to see if the eyes jerk distinctly which is a clue of impairment. Also, the officer is looking to see if the eyes jerk prior to a 45-degree angle, because onset of nystagmus prior to 45-degrees is another sign of impairment.

The driver taking the test has to be instructed to look straight ahead, and keep the head still while following and focusing on the stimulus until told to stop by the officer. The stimulus has to be about 12 to 15 inches in front of the driver's eyes for ease of focus and must be held at eye level, so that the eyes are wide open and looking directly at the stimulus. Police officers are trained to receive an acknowledgement from the driver that the stimulus is at a comfortable distance and to document this confirmation. Eyeglasses should be removed in order for the police officer to be able to make a more accurate determination of the driver's performance. If the person cannot see the stimulus without wearing eyeglasses, the test must be allowed wearing the glasses. Also, hard contact lenses should be removed to avoid any dislodging when the eyes are out at maximum deviation and to prevent damage to the eyes.

When administering the HGN test, the police look for three clues to determine if alcohol intoxication has taken place. The first clue that the police are looking for is the involuntary jerking of the eyes, also called the lack of smooth pursuit. Police officers are trained to look for the person's inability to pursue a stimulus smoothly while simultaneously focusing horizontally. If the driver moves his or her head at any time, the score may be invalid, regardless of which clue the officer is looking for. An example of smooth pursuit would be a marble rolling across a flat surface. If a driver is under the influence, the eyes will jerk as if the marble was rolled across a bumpy, uneven surface. The police officer is trained to check the left eye first by moving the stimulus to the officer's right. The stimulus has to be moved smoothly in order to be able to bring the driver's eye as far to the side as it can go. Any shaking hand movements by the officer could potentially induce nystagmus in the driver's eyes and possibly invalidate the test. Police are instructed to make two or more passes in front of the eye to be absolutely certain about the presence of nystagmus. If this clue is scored as nystagmus, the driver is assessed one point. However, just because the driver has this clue in one eye doesn't mean it will occur in the other eye.

The second clue the police are looking for is distinct jerkiness at maximum deviation. After the police officer has checked the first eye for smooth pursuit, the same eye has to be checked for distinct jerkiness at maximum deviation. The way the police perform this test is by moving the stimulus to the side until the eye has gone as far to the side as possible. When the eye is at this point, no sclera (white of the eye) will be visible in the corner of the eyeball. The eyeball must remain at that position for two or three seconds and for the police officer to attempt to discern eyeball jerkiness. If the police officer can't make this distinction from a slight nystagmus, the benefit of the doubt goes to the driver. A common mistake that police officers make is not bringing the eyes out to the side as far as they can go or too rapidly returning the stimulus. This can incorrectly score this part of the test. During this part of the test, a certain degree of discomfort is experienced, which causes a slight twitching of the eyes when they are at maximum deviation. If the police officer returns the stimulus too quickly, it can cause a natural nystagmus which can be mistaken for one caused by alcohol intoxication.

The third and final clue is what is referred to as the angle of onset. This clue is the most difficult to evaluate, but the angle of onset is perhaps the best indicator of the presence of the other clues. This correlation doesn't work conversely, however, the presence of either of the first two clues doesn't guarantee the third clue will be present. The driver will be told to follow the stimulus until they are looking down a 45-degree diagonal angle. To estimate this 45-degree angle, the police officer is told to place the stimulus between the driver's ear and nose on the side being tested. This estimation of the angle is critical because scientific studies have shown that as the intoxication of a person increases, the angle will decrease.

In order to score this part of the test, the police officer has to move the stimulus to a 45-degree angle so that the eye matches this angle. The police officer is looking for the eye to jerk during this movement. If nystagmus is observed, the officer will stop the stimulus and make note of the continued jerkiness. If the jerkiness does continue, the police officer must observe if there is still white showing in the corner of the eye. The officer will then note the angle as prior to 45 degrees. If there isn't any jerkiness, the stimulus has to continue until one of two things occurs: either the jerking occurs or the 45-degree angle is reached. If there isn't any white of the eye showing, the eye has probably been taken too far to the right, which would indicate maximum deviation. The other option as to why this occurred is because the person has unusual eyes that will not deviate very far to one side. The criteria of onset before 45 degrees can be used only if some white of the eye can be seen at the outside of the eye. Unfortunately, police officers often either incorrectly estimate the angle or score with no white showing in the corner of the eye. A question to ask is whether or not a police officer can hypothetically pick a 45-degree angle without having actual lines to use as a reference point. The angle of onset is deemed the most reliable in determining whether or not probable cause exists to believe that someone is under the influence of alcohol. Also, the angle of onset shouldn't be administered if the driver is lying down but can be given to a person who is sitting or standing.

The maximum number of clues in the HGN test in one eye is three. The total number for any driver is six (three for each eye). There is also the "vertical gaze nystagmus" test used to determine if a driver is under the influence of drugs. Vertical gaze nystagmus is the involuntary jerking of the eyes up and down which occur when the eyes look up at maximum elevation. The VGN test is sometimes given when it is presumed that the driver has ingested large amounts of alcohol or certain drugs.

There are three categories of nystagmus. "Rotational nystagmus" occurs when a person is spun around or rotated quickly, which causes the fluid in the inner ear to become disturbed. If the eyes of a person rotating were to be observed, they would be seen to jerk noticeably. "Post-rotational nystagmus" occurs when a person stops spinning because the fluid in the inner ear remains disturbed for a period of time, and the eyes continue to jerk. "Caloric nystagmus" occurs when fluid motion in the canals of the vestibular system is stimulated by temperature; for example, putting warm water in one ear and cold in the other.

There are a few conditions that can affect a gaze nystagmus test. A person who has a glass eye or vision in only one eye cannot be given this test for evaluation of just one eye with a doubled score. This assumes that the other eye would render the same results. If the person taking the test has what is known as a lazy eye, the officer is trained to test one eye while the person's other hand covers the other eye. A person with color blindness cannot take this test because nystagmus is common for the condition. A natural nystagmus may also present due to some form of neurological disorder, brain damage, epilepsy or pathological disorder. The narrowness of certain individuals' eyes can also make determination of nystagmus more difficult. A large disparity between the right and left eye is another indicator of a possible problem. If there is an accident, and the driver sustains a concussion, this can bring on pathological nystagmus which invalidates the test.

Police officers are trained to administer the HGN test with the driver facing a quiet, still background, turned away from police cruisers and any oncoming traffic. The reason for this is to avoid the possibility of inducing a condition known as optokinetic nystagmus. This develops when a person focuses on several objects at one time or on any objects that are moving away from the driver. Optokinetic nystagmus is a defense mechanism of the human body to prevent the eyes from tiring. There are numerous visual or other distractions that can also impede the results of the HGN test. Certain environmental factors such as wind, dust, rain, etc. can interfere with the performance of the nystagmus test. The law enforcement community considers the HGN test to be about 77 percent accurate when performed alone.

Some of the questions that need to be answered in relation to the HGN test are:

- Did the officer ask you to perform a test in which you were requested to follow a finger, pen, or some other object?
- What type of object did the officer use?
- What type of explanation, if any, was given to you about the test?
- What type of motion did the officer use to move the object?
- Did anything distract you while taking this test?
- How long did the test take?
- Did the officer comment on your performance?
- Do you have any medical issues with your eyes that could have impacted your performance on this test (i.e. astigmatism)?

Walk-and-Turn

The next field sobriety test is the walk-and-turn. This test, along with the next field sobriety test (the one-leg stand), is based upon the concept of divided attention. These tests divide the driver's attention between a physical task and a mental task. The physical tasks include balance and coordination while the mental tasks include comprehension of verbal instructions, recall of memory, and processing information. Divided attention tests are built around the idea that a person under the influence may be able to perform one task but not the other if under the influence of alcohol. These tests are designed to divide the driver's attention between two things at once to check for impairment because operating a motor vehicle requires divided attention.

The walk-and-turn test divides the driver's attention between balancing, counting out loud, recalling the number of steps, and turning - all according to the police officer's instructions. The correct administration of this test requires that it be performed on a hard, dry, level, non-slip surface with sufficient room for the driver to be able to complete nine heel-to-toe steps. Some of the issues with the validity of this test are when it is conducted in the winter with wind and weather conditions preventing proper standards of administration. DUI detection training calls for a straight line, which must be clearly visible. However, police officers are also taught that the test can be performed parallel to the curb provided the driver is in no physical danger. An officer may prevent the driver from taking the test or stop the test for safety reasons.

It needs to be stated that some people clearly shouldn't be given this test because even the average sober person would have difficulty performing it. Persons over the age of 65 or more than 50 pounds overweight will have increased difficulty. A person who has any physical impairment that would affect the ability to balance also should not be given this test. Police officers are trained to take medical issues into account when developing probable cause to make an arrest. Anyone, male or female, wearing heels more than two inches high should be given the opportunity to remove his or her shoes. The reason for this is obvious as an extended heel can affect a person's ability to balance and obstruct any validity to the test results. People who have vision issues such as not being able to see out of one eye may also have problems with this test because of poor depth perception.

The walk-and-turn test is comprised of two parts: the instructions stage and the walking stage. The instructions stage is designed to divide the driver's attention between balancing and listening to the police officer. The driver must stand with feet in the heel-to-toe position, keeping arms at the sides, all while listening to the police officer's instructions. The police officer needs to follow training and procedure perfectly during this stage, or it may affect the validity of the entire test. While the driver is taking this test, the police officer must observe the driver from approximately three to four feet away and remain motionless. If the police officer is too close or creates a distraction with excessive motion, this could cause the driver to make errors not made otherwise and decrease the validity of the test. The police officer has to give explicitly clear verbal instructions, supplemented with an actual demonstration of the test. Without the demonstration of the test, instructions alone can discredit the validity of the test results. The police officer has to receive affirmative confirmation of the driver's comprehension and understanding of the instructions. If the officer doesn't confirm the driver's understanding of the instructions each time an instruction is given, the results of the test may be invalid.

During the walking stage of the test, the police officer is trained to make sure that the right foot is in front of the left foot at the start of the test in order to maintain uniformity of procedure. This is also important later in the test when the driver has to turn and be evaluated on the turn. If a driver is instructed improperly, or shown an improper demonstration of the test, it could affect the test results. After getting into the starting position, the police officer has to inform the driver to remain in that position until told to begin walking. The officer has to demonstrate two or three heel-to-toe steps for the driver, as well as the difficult task of how to turn. The driver's foot has to be kept on the line and turning must be done by taking a series of small steps. The police officer will continue to instruct the driver to do the following:

- Keep your arms at your side while walking.
- Watch your feet at all times.
- Count your steps out loud.
- Don't stop once you have begun.

The walk-and-turn test relies on certain predictable mistakes that a person under the influence will display. It is a standardized field sobriety test, which means it follows the same procedure every time. There are also other scoring factors taken into consideration for failing or passing the test other than a subjective opinion. There are several ways that an officer can assess a point against a driver's performance. Officers are looking for eight specific clues:

Keeps balance during instructional phase: A point is scored against performance if the driver loses balance throughout the instructions only if the driver also doesn't maintain the heel-to-toe position. A point is not scored if the driver sways or uses arms to balance but maintains the starting position during this stage of the test.

Starts too soon: A point is scored when a driver starts to walk before the officer instructs him or her to do so. This can only be scored if the officer specifically instructed the driver not to start until told to do so and the driver stated that he or she understood the instruction. (I personally find this ironic, largely because the officer is starting to judge you immediately upon taking the first position. You can "start" the test too soon even though you are already being scored on the test!).

Stops while walking: A point can be scored if the driver stops to regain balance once the test starts. The police officer can't score this part of the test if the driver is simply walking too slowly, but can score this if the driver pauses for a few seconds after one step.

Doesn't touch heel to toe: If the driver leaves even a small space between the heel and the toe while walking, this point could be assessed.

Steps off line: The driver has to stay straight on the line or a point can be assessed, although this can happen more than once and only one point at maximum can be assessed.

Uses arms for balance: Police officers are trained to be conservative in their scoring and not to score a point if the driver sways or uses arms to balance.

Loses balance on turns or turns incorrectly: A driver can also be given a point if balance is lost during the turning part of the test. This point can be scored only if the driver takes both feet off the line while turning or doesn't take small steps. Also the driver cannot pivot in one movement, similar to the about-face used in military training. In order for scoring of the test to be proper, it is important that the police officer demonstrates and articulates the basis of movement to the driver.

Takes the wrong number of steps: This factor is only scored once, even if the wrong number of steps is taken in either direction.

During the whole process of the walk and turn, the driver has been instructed by the police to look down at his or her feet while counting the steps out loud. However, if a driver doesn't adhere to these instructions, a point cannot be scored because these are not scoring factors for the test.

If a driver receives at least two total points on the test, police officers are trained to use this as probable cause to believe that the driver is under the influence of alcohol and to make an arrest.

Police officers consider a driver unable to complete the walk-and-turn test when a driver does one of three things:

- Steps off line three or more times.
- Could potentially fall down.
- Simply cannot do the test.

Some questions relating to the walk-and-turn are:

- Did the officer specifically direct you to walk in a straight line for a certain number of steps?

- What directions did the officer give you before the test began?
- Did the officer demonstrate the test for you so you understood what was expected?
- How many steps did the officer take to demonstrate?
- What were you doing when the officer was explaining the test?
- Was there a line or some other identifiable marker for you to walk on while taking the test? If yes, what type of line was it, and how big was it?
- How long did the test take?
- How did you do on the test?
- Did the officer comment on your performance on this test?

Scientific studies consider the walk-and-turn test to be 68 percent accurate when administered alone. When combined with the HGN test, the pair is considered to be about 80 percent accurate in detecting impaired drivers.

One-Leg Stand

The final part of the field sobriety tests is the one-leg stand. It is a divided attention test that is based on two phases: the instructions phase and the balancing and counting phase. In order to accurately administer the one-leg stand, the police officer has to move the driver to a surface that is hard, dry, level, and non-slippery so that the driver would not be in any danger if he or she were to fall. Certain wind or weather conditions can interfere with the validity of this test. This test shouldn't be given to people who are more than 65 years old, more than 50 pounds overweight, or who have physical impairments that interfere with balance.

Anyone wearing high heels more than two inches high should be given the opportunity to remove his or her shoes as the heels may lower the reliability of the results. Police officers are not trained to give this test without adequate lighting. In darkness, even a sober person may have difficulty with the test. This is because there is a lack of a visual frame of reference that would otherwise be provided with proper lighting. Similar to the walk-and-turn test, it is important that the police officer observes the driver from at least three feet away. The police officer should also remain as motionless as possible so that there are absolutely no distractions caused.

In the administration of this test, there are two separate stages involved. The first phase is called the instructions phase. During the instructions phase, the driver has to stand with feet together, with arms at the sides, while listening to instructions. This is designed to divide the driver's attention between balancing and listening to the police officer's instructions. The test is begun by giving verbal instructions, followed by a demonstration. The police officer is trained to advise the driver to stand heels together and arms down at the sides, making sure not to begin the test until they are told to do so. The officer has to receive confirmation that the driver understood the instructions, and then document this acknowledgement. There aren't any scoring opportunities until the next stage of the test, which is the balance and counting stage. The only other possibility is if the driver can't perform the test, which would be scored as a maximum of four points and would be explained by the officer in the police report.

The next phase of the one-leg stand is the balancing and counting phase. At the beginning of this stage, the officer has to explain the test requirements further by instructing the driver to stand on one leg, and the driver is allowed to choose which leg to stand on. The driver has to hold the other foot in front about six inches from the ground, all the while keeping the foot parallel to the ground. While standing, the driver has to keep arms at the sides, and eyes on the elevated foot, while counting out loud "one thousand one, one thousand two", etc. all the way until a full 30 seconds has passed. This basically divides the driver's attention between balancing and counting.

The timing is important to note as impaired persons usually cannot stand for the full 30 seconds. Police officers are looking for four specific clues from drivers while they are performing the one-leg stand:

- Swaying while balancing.
- Using arms for balance.

- Hopping.
- Putting the foot down.

Police consider a driver unable to complete the one-leg stand when a driver either:

- Puts his/her foot down three or more times during the 30-second testing period, or
- Simply cannot do the test.

In regards to scoring the one-leg stand, a driver may be scored a point for swaying while balancing. Police officers are trained not to be too critical in regards to this scoring as the driver taking the test is not a gymnast and some swaying is a natural human reaction. The swaying that can be scored is a marked sway, which would be a back and forth motion while the driver maintains the position.

Another aspect of the scoring would be the driver using his or her arms for balance, raising them six or more inches from the side of the body. The police officer has to take into account the natural position of the arms. For example, some bodybuilders or men with large arms may have a natural position of more than six inches.

A third scoring factor on the test is whether or not a driver hops on one foot during the test. This is scored only if the driver resorts to hopping on the anchor foot in order to maintain balance. This point should not be scored if the driver is having difficulty by moving the anchor foot back and forth. As part of training, police officers are supposed to be able to distinguish this and to allow the driver this movement.

Finally, if the driver places his or her foot down, even if more than once, only one point can be given. The driver should be allowed to continue from the point of difficulty as the one-leg stand could lose sensitivity if it is repeated several times. The driver has to be instructed to keep watching the raised foot and to count out loud, but no points are issued if this instruction is not followed. If the driver counts too slowly, it is important that the officer stop the test after 30 seconds have elapsed as this could affect the scoring and validity of the test. Police officers are trained to time 30 seconds of total test time so if the driver counts too fast, the officer will instruct them to slow down.

A person can receive a maximum score on this test in two ways. The first way is if the driver puts the foot down three or more times during the 30-second count. The second way is if the driver can't perform the test because of his or her intoxication level. If this happens, the maximum score is given; however, police officers have to be able to articulate why they felt that the defendant was incapable. The one-leg stand administered alone is considered approximately 65 percent effective if instructed and scored properly.

For the purposes of the police report and any courtroom

testimony, the officer is trained that it is simply not enough to write the driver's score on the three tests. The numeric scores are only important to the police officer at the scene in order to establish probable cause. A score is insufficient to secure a criminal conviction in a court of law and has to be accompanied by more descriptive evidence. The police officer has to be able to describe in detail how the driver performed. Remember, once again, that you do not have to take the field sobriety tests and you can politely decline when the officer requests that you participate in the tests.

Some of the questions concerning the one-leg stand are:

- Did the officer ask you to stand on one leg?
- If the answer is yes, what directions did the officer give to you about this test before you began?
- Did the police officer specifically demonstrate this test for you?
- How long did the test take, specifically did you have to count to 30 or another number?
- How was your performance on this test?
- Did the officer comment on your performance on this test?

NON-STANDARDIZED FIELD SOBRIETY TESTS

There are also sobriety tests that are not yet validated but are used by police during DUI traffic stops. Counting backwards is a test that requires a person to count out loud a set of numbers in reverse order. For example, a driver is instructed to count out loud starting with the number 28 and go backwards until the number 14 is reached. This test divides the attention of the driver because it requires doing multiple things at once. As I have explained before, this is something that police officers are looking for to see if a person is under the influence. A person who is counting backwards has to remember what number to start with, count backwards correctly, and remember what number to stop on. The police view anything other than perfection as a sign of intoxication.

The alphabet test is a test that requires a person to recite a portion of the alphabet. An example of this test would be a driver being asked to start with a specific letter like C and told to stop at the letter Q. This test divides a person's attention because the person has to remember the specific letter to start with, recite the letters in sequence, and remember the letter to stop with. The police view anything less than perfection as a sign of alcohol intoxication.

One test that is still occasionally used is the finger count. This test is based upon the driver touching the tip of each finger in succession to the tip of the thumb, up and back, while counting the digits one, two, three, and four. The driver has to touch fingertips while not counting out of order. Anything less than perfection is seen by the police as a sign of alcohol intoxication.

Lastly, the stationary balance test requires a person to stand heels and toes touching, head back looking upward, and arms out to the side (like an airplane) for an estimated 30 seconds. The police officer is looking for any unnatural swaying. In our experience, we have had police officers testify that a range of anything from a half inch to an inch is too much sway and is a sign of intoxication. Also, if your estimation of the time period elapsed is more than 30 seconds, the police view this as a sign of intoxication.

Chapter 10:
The Breath Testing Device

In the State of Connecticut, breath-testing machines are used by law enforcement to test for the presence of alcohol after a driver has been arrested for DUI. These machines use infrared spectroscopy to identify molecules based on the way they absorb infrared light. Scientists discovered in the 20th century that all molecules are constantly vibrating, and these vibrations change when the molecules absorb infrared light. The changes in vibration include both the bending and stretching of various bonds. Each type of bond within a molecule absorbs infrared light at different wavelengths. Therefore, in order to identify ethanol in a sample, a scientist has to look at the wavelengths of the bonds in ethanol and measure the absorption of infrared light. The absorption wavelengths help to identify the substance as ethanol, and the amount of infrared absorption indicates how much ethanol is present.

The breath testing device has a cell where the driver exhales air into the device. There is an inlet for the cell and there is an exhaust portion of the cell, and a sample chamber through which the breath travels. The light source is similar to a regular light bulb that produces energy. It is the same type of energy that an electric stove emits and that one can feel when the burner turns red.

The breath testing device has a wheel at the outlet of the chamber where the light goes through and there are five different filters. The filters act similar to sunglasses. Each filter is different, and they filter out all unwanted light, allowing only small portions of light to come through. As the wheel goes around, small pulses of energy occur impacting the receptor as the filters break it up. The amount of heat that is sensed goes through what is referred to scientifically as an "A to D" (analog to digital) convert. The computer system inside doesn't automatically recognize that type of signal so it has to be converted to a digital signal first. It is then sent to a computer where it is reduced to a numerical value. That numerical value is then shown on a small screen on the face of the device and it prints out a readable result for the police. You should have a copy of the report. If the machine used is a Draeger Alcotest 9510 machine, the breath testing device results will be listed under the column "breath analysis" under the row subject "IR".

Breath analysis is based on the scientific law known as "Henry's law". Henry's law is officially defined as, "the mass of a gas that dissolves in a definite volume of liquid which is directly proportional to the pressure of the gas provided that the gas doesn't react with the solvent". In everyday, non-scientific language, this means that if a gas and liquid are in a closed container, the concentration of the gas in the air above the liquid is proportional to the concentration of the gas that is dissolved in the liquid. This can best be related to a thought experiment in which blood is in a closed container that contains alcohol. The alcohol will evaporate until the concentration in the air above the liquid is equal to that in the liquid. This is known as a fixed constant or "Henry's constant". The ratio given to that of the blood in the human body to be used in accordance with Henry's Law is 2100:1. This can best be explained as the concentration of alcohol in an average person's blood which is approximately 2100 times as great as the concentration in the air with it.

What this means is that if the alcohol concentration found in blood is in equilibrium with the alcohol in air, the alcohol concentration in the blood should be close to 2100 times greater. Problem is, there cannot be a normal status for the blood/air equilibrium because not every person has the same body weight, frame, and physical makeup. The ratio would be much wider depending upon the person being tested because the human body is not an ideal subject for a sealed container. Forensic scientists determined this problem of the "normal" ratio. There can be up to 0.03% error or more with a breath machine due to the normal ratio being used as a constant with the breath machine.

In addition to the issues of the ratio of the breath machine, the temperature of the individual supplying the sample can impact the reported results. What this means is that the temperature of the person taking the test could affect the results. A temperature increase of only two degrees Fahrenheit will cause about a 10 percent increase in BAC results due to the volatility of alcohol. Likewise, a drop in temperature can cause similar results. Also, a heavy dose of aspirin can cause body temperature to be reduced and thus potentially alter the results.

These two issues of breath can be used as a viable defense when being charged with a DUI. If you have taken any medication or have been sick, it is a good idea to tell the officer when they question you, or to later tell your attorney. If you have any medical conditions that could affect your normal blood ratio, you should let your attorney know so that they can obtain the correct medical documents to support your claims. If you are a diabetic, the police officer and your attorney should know because a diabetic can naturally produce ketones, which can skew the results of the breath test. A dedicated DUI attorney can review your medical history and investigate any possible medical defenses to the charges brought against you.

Chapter 11: Public Policy Reasoning for DUI Arrests

Each year in America, tens of thousands of people die in traffic accidents. Drivers that are impaired are more likely than other drivers to cause accidents. Drivers who are under the influence are less likely to wear seatbelts as well. Estimates are as high as two percent for the number of impaired drivers who are currently on the road at any given time.

Alcohol is a major contributor to traffic fatalities. In order to try to reduce the number of alcohol related injuries and accidents, police departments have used the policy of general deterrence to attempt to stop people from operating under the influence. This approach, supported by groups such as Mother's Against Drunk Driving, (MADD) is controversial and involves enforcement mechanisms including DUI checkpoints. The philosophical basis for general deterrence is to attempt to instill the fear of being arrested for DUI into the general public. In order to arrest a person and charge them with DUI, the driver has to be stopped first. A part of DUI law that you should know about is subsection 14-227f. Public pressure on both the State's Attorney's Office and the state legislature in Connecticut by groups like MADD is incredibly strong. This section of the DUI law reads that a prosecutor must state - in open court - why a DUI charge is being reduced or dismissed. As a result of this, many prosecutors will not reduce or drop a DUI case. They would much rather go to trial, even if it is not a very strong case, because of the potential career implications.

Chapter 12: Defenses

Often, I am asked if it is possible to defend against a DUI charge. The answer to the question is that like most problems in the practice of law, it depends on the facts, circumstances, and issues of each particular case. A defense that could work well in one case might not work in another. In our experience, we prefer to alter our strategy depending upon the case at hand. For example, if I have a case where there is a chain-of-custody issue with a piece of important evidence, such as a blood sample, I will focus on that issue. I would rather have one very strong issue to work with than something irrelevant, such as a police officer writing down that the car was a 4-door instead of a 2-door.

Some of the best defenses to use are legal defenses that are based on case precedent. A person could be clearly intoxicated, and probably unsafe to operate a motor vehicle, but if a police officer makes a stop without an articulable reason why, the judge has to suppress evidence derived from an illegal traffic stop. I will explain some of the more common defenses in DUI cases.

To convict a person of DUI, the state has to prove beyond a reasonable doubt that a defendant was driving a vehicle. This means that the prosecutor has to prove that you (and not someone else) were the driver of a vehicle. Some of the issues that are often contested in a case in relation to operation of a motor vehicle are where the vehicle was found, whether the keys were in the ignition, whether the motor vehicle was running, whether the vehicle was operable, whether the defendant was conscious, etc. If you were passed out, for example, with the vehicle running at a stoplight, a jury might find this to be "driving". If, however, you were in your driveway using your car for shelter, a jury might not find this to be driving, regardless of your intoxication level.

When challenging the impairment of a driver, the prosecutor is required to prove that the driver was substantially incapable of operating a motor vehicle safely because of the consumption of alcohol. In order to vote guilty, a jury has to unanimously believe, beyond a reasonable doubt, that a defendant's ability to drive was affected by alcohol or drug consumption. If a driver can safely operate a vehicle without swerving, weaving, speed variations, or showing signs of impairment, these facts go towards reasonable doubt. This type of defense is used in cases in which a defendant is pulled over by the police for an infraction such as speeding, which is not necessarily indicative of operating under the influence.

For example, if a driver being pulled over for a taillight violation doesn't show signs of operating under the influence when responding to the officer's lights to pull over, it could be reasonable to believe that prior alcohol or drug consumption didn't impair him or her at the time of driving. Another defense is to challenge the test result, whether blood, breath, or urine. Certain factors and circumstances can prevent a breath testing device from obtaining an accurate reading. An example of something that can alter a breath testing device reading would be contaminating substances in the machine that can be mistaken for alcohol molecules and ultimately cause a false result. Human error can also contribute to the accuracy of the test results.

It is important to know that some DUI cases are difficult to defend. Part of effective legal representation involves extensive negotiating for a better result for the client before trial. Our focus on some cases, especially those involving accidents with a victim, is mitigation and getting the least restrictive sentence possible. Even cases that look difficult can get a good result, depending upon a number of circumstances that may not be easily recognizable. It is always necessary to explore all of the various legal and factual defenses to get the best possible result, regardless of whether or not the case goes to trial.

Chapter 13:
Plea Bargains

Most DUI cases in the criminal justice system tend to be resolved by way of a plea agreement prior to a trial. Before a trial takes place, there is a negotiation process that takes place between the prosecutor and your defense attorney, if you are represented. For some criminal charges, the prosecutor will agree to reduce or dismiss some or even all of the charges, usually in exchange for a guilty plea to some other or lesser charge.

It needs to be first noted that DUI is a hot-button political issue every year in the Connecticut State Legislature. The DUI laws have grown more severe over time and have no signs of being reduced in severity. Members of the legislature are elected by the general public and not a month goes by in Connecticut without news of a fatal motor vehicle accident involving alcohol. Legislators are deeply concerned with public opinion and in Connecticut, prosecutors are not interested in reducing or dismissing DUI charges.

It should be known that there is no constitutional right to a plea bargain. What this means is that the prosecutor never has to make a plea offer to a defendant. Therefore, you have no constitutional right to an offer, but most of the time, the prosecutor will make one as an alternative to trial. This is what is called a "plea offer". If you accept the plea offer, and the judge accepts the plea offer, your case is now resolved in what is called a "plea bargain". The State's Attorney and your defense attorney will discuss your case and the State's Attorney will convey an offer to your attorney. This offer can get better or worse during the course of your case, and can even be revoked at any time.

The decision whether or not to go to trial or accept a plea offer is the defendant's decision to make. A defense attorney has the responsibility to communicate this offer to the defendant, and can recommend legally what he or she thinks is the best course of action. However, only a defendant can decide whether or not to accept an offer. Before considering your offer, I can counsel you on the positives, negatives, and consequences of the plea offer, rather than a trial. Depending upon the circumstances of your case, it may be in your best interest to accept a plea offer, rather than proceed to trial. If the likelihood of success at trial is incredibly slim, there may be substantial benefit to you accepting an offer.

When making an offer to you, the prosecutor is usually

not emotionally moved by what kind of outstanding citizen you are in your local community. Even if you have no prior DUIs, or even a traffic ticket, fully expect that the prosecutor will not be willing to dismiss or reduce the charges against you in a DUI case. Whether or not you should accept a plea bargain in your case ultimately depends upon the facts and circumstances of your case. In some cases, for instance, your personal desire to stay out of jail can be conveyed to the prosecutor and a resolution based around that desire could hopefully be reached.

Often, the first plea offer that is received from the prosecutor is the best one. A factor to consider when deciding to accept an offer is your goals in their priority order of importance. If staying out of jail is your top priority, you need to communicate this to your attorney. There are collateral consequences to a criminal conviction such as the potential loss of a job. Losing your driver's license is a consideration as well, because for many it is necessary in order to get to work, school, etc. If you have a professional license, such as a law license, nursing, medicine, etc. you should tell your attorney right away. In trying to craft the best solution to your case, your attorney must be apprised of all of the various factors and circumstances about who you are, both personally and professionally.

In order to determine whether to go to trial, the likelihood of success is the biggest factor. If there isn't much of a chance of a good result at trial, there usually isn't much of a reason to go to trial unless there is a lack of reasonable offers from the prosecution. If your case is one with strong defenses, it is likely that the prosecutor will make you a much more appealing offer because the State will see the weaknesses of the case. Some of those weaknesses could be the potential violation of your constitutional rights during the initial traffic stop.

If you do accept a plea bargain and come to an agreement with the prosecuting attorney in your case, you will have to stand before the judge in your case and accept the plea offer formally in court. This acceptance can happen at any stage of the proceedings, but the judge has to make you answer questions to be absolutely sure that you understand your rights before you give them up and move forward.

When accepting a plea offer, the judge will ask you questions such as if the plea offer is a disposition that you are willing to accept. The judge will go over your trial rights and make sure you understand what you are giving up by accepting the plea offer. The judge will want to confirm with you that no one has put any influence or pressure on you to plead guilty, and that this guilty plea is freely and voluntarily given. It also has to be a plea that is not under the influence of any drugs, medications, or alcohol that would impair your ability to make a rational decision.

To sum up, whether or not to accept a plea offer in your DUI case depends upon the facts and circumstances of your case. There isn't a specific rule or guideline in determining how to best pursue a DUI case. The experience, skill, and diligence of your defense attorney can help, and he or she can make a recommendation as to the best way to pursue your case. Based upon the positives and negatives of your case, along with the unique circumstances of every DUI case, hopefully you can acquire an acceptable resolution.

Chapter 14:
Automobile Insurance Issues

It is important for you to understand that your insurance company for your motor vehicle is assessing you on multiple factors to determine the premium that you will pay. Automobile insurers use scoring that includes credit card data when they determine your automobile insurance policy premium rates. Your credit reports put you into a class system to determine your pricing tier. Insurers make their decisions on a correlation between the scores determined for customers and the probability that a customer will file a claim.

If you have been arrested for a DUI, it will directly impact your insurance score. You can realistically expect to pay hundreds more a year for your first DUI offense and much more for consecutive offenses. Many insurance companies check your motor vehicle history only once every three years or when a person is applying for a new policy. Sometimes accidents, tickets, and drunk driving convictions escape your insurer's attention. However, if your insurer does find out about a DUI conviction or driver's license suspension, you are likely to have your rates raised and possibly even have your policy cancelled.

There are basically two ways that insurance companies deal with customers who have been convicted of DUI. The first way is that the insurer will likely raise the insurance premium and label you a high-risk driver. In this case, you will likely have to provide proof of insurance for up to five years with the State of Connecticut DMV. Your insurance company will have to provide the DMV with an SR-22 form, which removes your license suspension by providing the State with proof of insurance. An SR-22 form also means your insurance carrier is required to notify the DMV if it cancels your insurance for any reason. Also, your insurance company may cancel your insurance mid-term or terminate the policy at the end of the term because you are currently in a preferred class. Your insurance company will send you a notice stating why you have been cancelled, and then you will have to find another car insurer while having a cancellation on your claim history.

Some insurance companies don't offer SR-22 policies, so you may also be non-renewed or cancelled because your insurance policy can no longer provide what you need. Insurers can miss DUI convictions sometimes and it is possible that your insurance company will never find out about your conviction, especially if you don't have to get an SR-22. Keep in mind that insurance rates don't always go up. You might be surprised to know that when your insurer does find out about a DUI conviction, it doesn't automatically impose higher premiums. The insurer will look at your history with the company and your claims record when making their decision.

Chapter 15:
Drug Related DUI

When most people think of DUI, they think of drunk driving. However, not all DUI arrests are the result of intoxication due to alcohol. Driving under the influence also refers to driving with drugs in your system. If you have been arrested for a DUI because the police officer believes that you were operating a motor vehicle while impaired by drugs, you need to understand how your drug DUI differs from the more common alcohol-related DUI. In this chapter, I will discuss the drug DUI law, common misconceptions when it comes to this form of DUI, field and lab detection, and defenses that I can use to help you in this situation.

Connecticut's General Statute section 14-227a claims that, "No person shall operate a motor vehicle while under the influence of intoxicating liquor or any drug or both. A person commits the offense of operating a motor vehicle while under the influence of intoxicating liquor or any drug or both if such person operates a motor vehicle (1) while under the influence of intoxicating liquor or any drug or both, or (2) while such person has an elevated blood alcohol content. For the purposes of this section, "elevated blood alcohol content" means a ratio of alcohol in the blood of such person that is eight-hundredths of one per cent or more of alcohol, by weight, except that if such person is operating a commercial motor vehicle, "elevated blood alcohol content" means a ratio of alcohol in the blood of such person that is four-hundredths of one per cent or more of alcohol, by weight, and "motor vehicle" includes a snowmobile and all-terrain vehicle, as those terms are defined in section 14-379." Note that the statute claims that driving under the influence of "intoxicating liquor *or any drug*" is grounds for a DUI.

The state of Connecticut considers both illegal and legal drugs to be impairing when it comes to operating a motor vehicle. This means that the DUI law treats driving under the influence of cocaine the same as it treats driving under the influence of prescribed sleeping pills. Some common drugs that you can be arrested for consuming and driving include:

- Antidepressants.
- Antihistamines.
- Cocaine.
- Decongestants.
- Heroin.
- Hydrocodone.
- LSD.

- Marijuana.
- Methamphetamine.
- Morphine.
- Sleeping pills.
- Valium.

You can even be arrested for a drug DUI if it is found that you have caffeine or nicotine in your system.

THE RISE OF PRESCRIPTION PILLS

Prescription pill use and abuse has increased dramatically in recent years. Prescription pill abuse has increased in two main age groups – people in their late teens and early twenties, and elderly people.

There is no doubt that prescription pills are given with fewer restrictions today than they were 50 years ago. Many children and teens are prescribed medication for disorders such as ADD, ADHD, bipolar disorder, and depression. Some high school and college students have found that they can do better in school when they abuse their prescription pills. These students might also find that they can make a profit by selling extra pills that they have obtained through an ongoing prescription or a prescription for pain medication after surgery.

The other age group that has seen an explosion in prescription pill abuse is the elderly. In many cases, this abuse is inadvertent, as it can be difficult to keep track of multiple medications, which pills you can or cannot use if you are consuming alcohol, etc. Now that the Baby Boomer generation is reaching retirement, more and more people are prescribed pills. Because of the number of elderly people using prescription pills, prescription pill abuse – inadvertent or not – has increased.

In many cases, prescription pill labels warn users not to operate a motor vehicle or heavy machinery for a certain number of hours after taking the medication, because the medication will impair the user's judgment and motor skills. This can lead to signs of driving under the influence, such as driving at a speed that is too fast or too slow, swerving in and out of lanes, cutting off other drivers, etc. If a police officer sees you exhibiting this behavior while you are operating a motor vehicle, he or she will pull you over and try to determine if you are driving under the influence.

A common misconception when it comes to prescribed medication is that if you have a prescription, you cannot be arrested for driving while under the influence of this medication. Prescription or no prescription, if you are driving recklessly due to medication that you have been taking, you can be arrested for a DUI. Because many prescription bottles warn users not to drive under the influence of the medication, the fact that the medication was prescribed is not a valid argument. This is the determination that the state of Connecticut came to in the case of *State v. Borrelli.* In this case, a woman was arrested for a DUI after taking prescribed anti-depressants, anti-anxiety medication, and over-the-counter allergy medication (Benadryl and Tavist-D). The combination of medication made her lethargic and caused her to drive erratically on the road. The court determined that even though she was taking medication that was prescribed to her and basic, over-the-counter medicine, she was still guilty of a DUI because she was aware that she was not in a proper state to drive, and she endangered others by driving at that time. Please keep in mind that you can be arrested for driving under the influence of prescription pills if the medication causes reckless driving. Similarly, if you have a card for medical marijuana, you can still be arrested for a drug DUI if it is determined that there is THC in your system while you are driving.

Another common misconception when it comes to drug DUIs is that having a drug in your system will impact your ability to drive. While the use of drugs can cause you to drive recklessly or in an unsafe manner, not all drugs affect motor skills. For example, caffeine, nicotine, and even marijuana might not affect your motor skills to the extent of causing dangerous driving. A good DUI lawyer can help you make the case that even though you were under the influence of drugs, this did not affect your driving in a negative way.

ROADSIDE DETECTION

Since 1979, United States police officers have been using the Unvalidated and Uncorrelated Drug Recognition Evaluation and the drug examination to determine what drug is causing impairment in someone driving under the influence. Today, the International Association of Chiefs of Police (IACP) is in charge of the Drug Examination and Classification Program (DECP). This program is used in over 37 states, including the state of Connecticut. Police officers can be accepted into the DRE program even if they don't have a formal education or basic knowledge of medicine and science. Despite the minimal prerequisites, upon completing the DRE training, police officers are considered proficient in drug classification and distinction. The following are the requirements for admission into the expert Drug Recognition School:

- At least a year of participation in law enforcement.
- Completion of a probationary period.
- Having above average knowledge in DUIs.
- Certification in standardized field sobriety testing.
- A recommendation from the DRE coordinator of the officer's department.

DRE examinations occur roadside when a police officer suspects that a driver is under the influence of a drug. There are twelve steps in the process. They are:

Step 1: Breath Alcohol Test. This test is administered to try to determine the driver's blood alcohol content (BAC) level.

Step 2: Interview of the Arresting Officer. If the DRE officer is not the arresting officer, the DRE officer is required to inform the arresting officer of what he or she has observed. In many cases, information is lost or misconstrued during this process. This can become a weakness in the prosecution's case that a good drug DUI defense attorney can exploit.

Step 3: Initial Exam and First Pulse. A DRE officer will begin an exam by asking the driver questions in order to determine if the driver has a medical condition or disease that might be interpreted as a form of drug impairment. At this point, the DRE officer should be wearing latex gloves. Once the latex gloves are put on, the officer should take the driver's pulse. If latex gloves are not worn during the first pulse, the results can be inaccurate. In fact, the whole DRE examination might be determined inaccurate if proper procedure is not followed during this or any of the other steps. Even a small inconsistency such as not wearing latex gloves can have a big impact on the DRE exam.

Step 4: Eye Exam. A three-part eye examination should be administered next. The DRE officer should be checking for lack of convergence, horizontal gaze nystagmus, and vertical gaze nystagmus.

Step 5: Divided Attention Psychophysical Test. Four field tests will be administered at this time: the Romberg balance test, the one-legged stand test, the nine-step walk and turn test, and the finger to nose test.

Step 6: Vital Signs and Second Pulse. The driver's vitals should be taken at this time, including blood pressure, body temperature, and a second check of the driver's pulse.

Step 7: Dark Room Exam. The driver's eyes should next be examined in a dark room. The DRE officer should check for pupil size, the pupil's reaction to light, rebound dilation, and other factors of how the eyes change in the dark room. The officer is attempting to observe how the pupils change and correlate this change to drug classification.

Step 8: Exam of Muscle Tone. Muscle tone should be determined by having the DRE officer grab the driver's upper arm and check for normal, flaccid, or rigid muscle tone.

Step 9: Checking for Injection Sites and Third Pulse. A third check of the driver's pulse should be administered at this time. In addition, the officer should search for track or needle marks on the driver's vein lines.

Step 10: Driver's Statement. The DRE officer will try to get a confession from the driver at this stage in the process.

Step 11: Analysis by the Evaluator. The DRE officer should form an opinion on the sobriety of the driver at this point. If the officer believes that the driver is under the influence of a drug, he or she has to determine what drug category the impairment is under. The categories are:

- Analogs.
- Cannabis.
- CNS Depressants.
- CNS Stimulants.
- Hallucinogens.
- Inhalants.
- PCP.

Step 12: Toxicological Exam. The DRE officer's opinion and analysis will be substantiated or refuted by a chemical sample from the driver.

The major issue with the DRE exam and The Unvalidated and Uncorrelated Drug Recognition Evaluation is that they do not have to be very effective to be considered accurate or acceptable when arresting someone for a drug DUI. Incredibly, an officer or certified drug recognition examiner only has to be 28% correct when determining the drug causing the impairment in order to arrest the driver. Clearly, the Unvalidated and Uncorrelated Drug Recognition Evaluation is not very accurate, yet it is used as a factor in arresting drivers who are under the influence. In addition, it does not take much to become a DRE certified officer. As I've stated above, there are simply basic requirements such as a recommendation for the program, a time requirement as a law enforcement agent, and knowledge of DUI. Eligible police officers just have to complete an academic and a field phase in order to get the knowledge and experience to perform the DRE examination. Many feel that additional training is required to accurately and properly administer this test and interpret the results. Sometimes, the DRE examination is not administered correctly. If this is the case in your situation, your DUI defense lawyer should exploit these issues. Ultimately, a good DUI lawyer might be able to ensure that the DRE exam results are inadmissible in court.

Another way to test for drug impairment is through the use of an oral fluid drug test. An oral fluid drug test works by analyzing the saliva in a driver's mouth. The device works by using an absorbent collection device to collect and screen saliva.

One pro of using the oral fluid drug test as opposed to a urine test is that the driver can collect the sample him or herself and give it to the officer. This can prevent tampering with samples and ensure that the drug test is accurate. In addition, collecting a sample this way is less invasive than other options, and it is simpler to standardize and perform. Compared to other types of drug tests, such as urine tests, the oral fluid test is more accurate. This is because an oral fluid test can detect drugs in the driver's system right after the drug is used, instead of having to wait for it to be metabolized for a urine sample.

Laboratory Detection

In addition to roadside tests, such as the DRE

examination and the oral fluid test, drug detection can take place in the lab through standard blood and urine tests, as well as gas chromatography-mass spectrometry (GC-MS) tests. The GC-MS test is a common method of drug testing in the laboratory. It uses a combination of the gas chromatography and the mass spectrometry test to ensure a high level of accuracy. In the GC-MS process, first an immunoassay or initial test is performed. If this immunoassay comes back negative, no additional testing will be done. However, if the immunoassay test is positive, an additional test will be performed. This is the confirmatory GC-MS test. This test can determine specific types and quantities of drugs that the driver may have in his or her system. The GC-MS or a similar confirmatory test should be used before a drug test can be confirmed as positive.

Many feel that the GC-MS test is the most accurate device that is used in the laboratory to detect drugs. The power of this device comes from the fact that it gathers multiple forms of information. Retention time, ions, and a spectrum are all collected from the GC-MS system.

DEFENSES

If you have been charged with a drug DUI, it is important to understand that this does not automatically mean that you will be convicted of one. With the help of a DUI lawyer experienced in drug DUI, defenses can be raised to help fight your DUI. It is important to keep in mind that not all defenses will work for every drug DUI case. You should discuss your personal situation with an attorney before making a decision on the best defense for you. Regardless, here are some common drug DUI defenses.

Tolerance

Just because you have drugs in your system does not mean that you are guilty of driving recklessly. If you are taking prescribed medication, or if you have a high tolerance to a particular drug, it may not affect you in any way. You may be used to the drug, having built up resilience to it. If, for example, you have ingested a small dosage of the drug, you may be able to drive just fine.

No impact of motor skills

Driving under the influence of a drug does not automatically mean that your motor skills will be impacted. For example, most people can safely operate a vehicle if they have had one or two alcoholic beverages due to the fact that a small amount of alcohol will not significantly impact motor skills. Likewise, some drugs do not alter motor skills or judgment, and will not cause you to drive in an unsafe manner. You can make this argument in a court of law if you have been charged with a drug DUI.

Because drug DUIs are less common than alcohol DUIs,

only a limited number of Connecticut DUI defense lawyers can truly give you the drug DUI defense that you need. We have special training in drug DUIs and Jay is the only lawyer in Connecticut with GC-MS certification. For the best defense for your drug DUI, please contact us at your convenience.

Chapter 16:
Pretrial Alcohol Education Program

A driver charged with DUI may apply for admission to the Pretrial Alcohol Education Program. As a result of the Connecticut State Legislature enacting such stiff penalties, a statute was passed creating the Alcohol Education Program. If a defendant successfully completes the program, which includes a series of educational lectures, it will result in a dismissal of the case by the Court. It should be understood that this program is not open to every person charged with DUI. The alcohol education classes are administered by private agencies, and the State will make defendants pay the fee. Currently, the fee is $200, which is paid to the court to cover the costs of your evaluation by the Department of Mental Health & Addiction Services. After your evaluation, you return to court in a few weeks and if they agree, the judge will assign you to attend a number of classes for an additional fee of $350 to $500.

Applicants to the program will have to make affirmations under oath before a judge, including statements that they have not used the program within the past 10 years (or never, if under the age of 21). A major benefit of the program is that the court seals the file when a driver applies for the program. The court can grant the application after considering any recommendations from the State's Attorney. If the court does grant the application, the driver's license suspension remains in effect; however, the driver has the option of not starting the program until the end of the license suspension period.

The evaluator can also recommend intensive outpatient or inpatient treatment, which is paid directly to the provider. Successful completion will entitle you to a dismissal of the case against you. A dismissal means that no record of the arrest would be kept. The only thing that will remain after a dismissal is a notation on your driving history that you were in the program. This may or may not have insurance implications, but that depends on your insurance carrier and your prior record. It should be noted that one of the strengths of this program for our clients is that they do not admit guilt. In fact, many of our clients who strongly feel that they are not guilty use this program as a way to avoid going to trial and paying for a trial. In a way, it allows the case to "go away" with minimal impact on their life. Most importantly, current law allows you to use this program every 10 years.

If you decide to choose this program, it is easiest to have cash on hand; the Clerk of the Court accepts MasterCard, Visa, cash or personal check as long as the address on your check matches the address on your license. The fee must be paid the same day as the court appearance. This option is a pretrial program, and most judges will not let you apply after your case has been added to the jury list, so it is important to consider this option before choosing not to use it. Note that if a driver was involved in an accident that caused a serious physical injury or if the DUI charge resulted from operating a commercial motor vehicle, the driver is ineligible for the program. As of January 1, 2014, CDL holders are no longer eligible for the program.

Reinstatement to the program is possible if a person didn't successfully complete the assigned program or is no longer amenable to treatment. The program provider has to recommend to the court whether the individual would best be served by:

- A 10-session intervention program.
- A 15-session intervention program.
- Placement in a state-licensed substance abuse treatment program.

In Conclusion

Thank you for reading our book. We sincerely hope that this book has given you a much clearer understanding of what happens in the process of dealing with a DUI in Connecticut. As you can plainly see, there are a variety of issues involved in successfully defending a DUI charge in a court of law. Despite the constant erosion of our Constitutional rights as citizens of the United States by the government, there are viable defenses to being accused of driving under the influence. Only after looking at all of the information available can attorneys like us make a determination as to how to best handle a case. Keep in mind that every case, like every client, is unique and we encourage you to play an active role in your defense, starting with consulting with an experienced DUI lawyer.

We are proud of our reputation as some of the best criminal defense attorneys in Connecticut – it has been gained by fighting for our clients, day in and day out. We do whatever we possibly can to help our clients. We strongly encourage you to not be pessimistic during the legal process; it is often frightening, demoralizing and complicated. Always stay optimistic, positive and hopeful that justice will be in your favor. Please contact our law office to discuss your concerns, questions, and the circumstances of your arrest. Remember, most importantly, that hope is not a strategy in a court of law, but having us on your side is.

Frequently Asked Questions

Q: Should I take or refuse the breath test?

A: Unfortunately, there isn't a single correct answer to this question. The proper choice depends upon the unique facts relating to your case. As stated previously, the punishment for someone who has no prior Connecticut DUI suspensions of the driver's license is going to depend upon the breath testing device results. If you submit to the test, you will need to have the IID installed in your vehicle for 6 months following the 45 day suspension. If you refuse the test, the IID period following the 45 day suspension will be 1 year.

Q: What should I do immediately following my DUI arrest?

A: Generally, the most important thing to do is to get in contact with an attorney - the sooner the better. The days and weeks following an arrest are stressful. In order to get the best possible legal outcome, it is crucial to get in contact with an attorney who can explain what is occurring and how to manage your case.

Q: What court will hear my case?

A: The State of Connecticut is divided up into Judicial Districts; the courthouse assigned to you is based upon the geographical location of the incident and arrest.

Q: I had a prior DUI in another state and either used a program or was convicted. Will the State of Connecticut know about it?

A: Likely, the answer to this question is 'yes'. The local State's Attorney's Office will run an extensive criminal background check on you as part of their procedures.

Q: Could this case affect a professional license?

A: Yes. If you hold a professional license such as a license to practice law, medicine, nursing, engineering, or accounting you should be concerned about the fact that an alcohol or drug-related conviction could require reporting to your professional licensing board and possible further action.

Q: The police officers didn't read me my Miranda rights. Is there anything that can be done?

A: Maybe, largely because Miranda rights are triggered when a person is in custody and responding to questions asked by law enforcement officers. Before questioning a person, a police officer has to warn the driver that anything they say can be used against them in court, and that they have a right to speak with an attorney before answering questions.

Q: If my license is suspended by the DMV, and I am caught

driving under suspension, what are the consequences?

A: If you are caught by the police operating a motor vehicle under suspension, the mandatory minimum is thirty days in jail.

Made in the USA
Monee, IL
04 November 2026

67385814R10085